Spiritual Maladies

Spiritual Maladies is translated from the French published by Éditions Olivétan as *Les maladies de la vie spirituelle*.

In the same collection of translations:

The Silence of God during the Passion
Praying the Psalms
Repentance—Good News!
The Tenderness of God
Becoming a Disciple
From Darkness to Light

Spiritual Maladies

Daniel Bourguet

Foreword by Bob Ekblad

Translated from the French

CASCADE *Books* • Eugene, Oregon

SPIRITUAL MALADIES

English translation copyright © 2016 Wipf and Stock Publishers. All rights reserved. Except for brief quotations in critical publications or reviews, no part of this book may be reproduced in any manner without prior written permission from the publisher. Write: Permissions, Wipf and Stock Publishers, 199 W. 8th Ave., Suite 3, Eugene, OR 97401.

Translated from the original French edition.
Copyright © 2000 Éditions Olivétan, Lyon, France.

Cascade Books
An Imprint of Wipf and Stock Publishers
199 W. 8th Ave., Suite 3
Eugene, OR 97401

www.wipfandstock.com

PAPERBACK ISBN: 978-1-4982-8182-9
HARDCOVER ISBN: 978-1-4982-8184-3
EBOOK ISBN: 978-1-4982-8183-6

Cataloguing-in-Publication data:

Names: Bourguet, Daniel.

Title: Spiritual maladies / Daniel Bourguet.

Description: Eugene, OR: Cascade Books, 2016 | Includes bibliographical references.

Identifiers: ISBN 978-1-4982-8182-9 (paperback) | ISBN 978-1-4982-8184-3 (hardcover) | ISBN 978-1-4982-8183-6 (ebook)

Subjects: LSCH: 1. Spiritual healing | 2. Healing—religious aspects | 3. Sin |

Classification: BL65. B47 B20 2016 (print) | BL65. B47 (ebook)

Manufactured in the USA.   08/31/16

Contents

Translator's Note | vi
Foreword by Bob Ekblad | vii
Preface | xiii
Introduction | xv

1 God the Physician | 1
2 A Divine Consultation | 26
3 The Fathers' Medicine | 64

The Prayer of Bartimaeus | 89

Translator's Note

IN SOME INSTANCES THERE are idioms in French that are difficult to translate, but that has not generally been the case with this book. Further to the author's original notes some translator's notes have been added as footnotes, generally as glosses of the French, sometimes of a more explanatory nature; in every instance these notes have been checked with the author. Biblical passages are mostly the translator's version of the French since at times the point would be lost if this were not so; the author chooses freely among French translations.

Foreword

THE PUBLICATION OF DANIEL Bourguet's books in English is a valuable contribution to the literature of contemplative theology and spirituality that will nourish and inspire the faith of all who read them. Daniel Bourguet, a French Protestant pastor and theologian of the Huguenot tradition, lives as a monk in the mountainous Cévennes region in the South of France. There at his hermitage near Saint-Jean-du-Gard, Daniel maintains a daily rhythm of prayer, worship, Scripture reading, theological reflection, and spiritual accompaniment. All of his books flow out of a life steeped in love of God, Scripture, and the seekers who come to him for spiritual support.

I first met Daniel Bourguet in 1988 when my wife, Gracie, and I moved from rural Central America to study theology at the Institut Protestant de Théologie (IPT), where he taught Old Testament. The IPT is the Église protestante unie de France's[1] denominational graduate school in Montpellier, France.

Prior to our move to France while ministering among impoverished farmers in Honduras in the 1980s, we had come across the writings of Swiss theologian Wilhelm Vischer and French theologian Daniel Lys by way of footnotes in Jacques Ellul's inspiring books. Vischer had written a three-volume work entitled *The Witness of the Old Testament to Christ*, of which only volume 1 is translated into English.[2]

1. Then the Église réformée de France.
2. Wilhelm Vischer, *The Witness of the Old Testament to Christ*, vol. 1, *The*

That book, along with a number of articles and Daniel Lys's brilliant *The Meaning of the Old Testament*,[3] exposed us to a community of Bible scholars who articulated a continuity between the Old and New Testaments that was highly relevant then and now. This connection would ultimately lead me to Bourguet.

We experienced firsthand how a literal reading of the Old Testament in isolation from the New Testament confession that Jesus is both Lord and Christ (Messiah) brings great confusion, division, and even destruction. In rural Honduras churches often distinguish themselves by selective observance of Old Testament laws and use of certain Old Testament stories to inspire fear of God as punishing judge. In North America Christians were drawing from the Old Testament to justify the death penalty and US military intervention in Central America and beyond.

Wilhelm Vischer himself had been an active resister of Nazism from his Old Testament teaching post inside Germany. He resisted the misuse of Scripture to justify anti-Semitism, nationalism, and war, insisting on the importance of the Old Testament for Christian faith at a time when it was being dismissed. He was consequently one of the first professors of theology to be pressured to leave his post and eventually depart Nazi Germany before World War II, and served as Karl Barth's pastor in Basel after he too left Germany. After the war, the church in France, having been widely engaged in resistance to Nazism and deeply encouraged by Barth, invited Vischer to be the professor of Old Testament at the IPT in Montpellier.

Ellul, Vischer, Lys, and other French theologians were offering deep biblical reflection that led us to look into theological study in France.[4] We wrote the IPT about their graduate program and

---

Pentateuch, trans. A. B. Crabtree (London: Lutterworth, 1949).

3. Daniel Lys, *The Meaning of the Old Testament* (Nashville: Abingdon, 1967).

4. We were able to study with pastor and New Testament professor Michel Bouttier, who was also trained by Vischer and published broadly, including a commentary on Ephesians and a number of collections of provocative articles. Elian Cuvillier followed Michel Bouttier and is currently Professor of New Testament at

Foreword

discovered that Vischer had long since retired after training several generations of pastors. His protégée, Daniel Lys, had recently retired but was still available. In Lys's place was his doctoral student Daniel Bourguet, who also had been trained by Vischer. The IPT welcomed us with a generous scholarship and we were soon making plans to learn French and move to Montpellier.

We were eager for help to understand Scripture after being immersed in Bible studies with impoverished farmers in war-torn Honduras. Disillusioned with America after being engaged in resisting US policy in Central America, we felt drawn to reflect from a different context. We reasoned that studying in a Protestant seminary with a history of persecution in a majority Catholic context would prove valuable. We left Tierra Nueva in the hands of local Honduran leaders and moved to Montpellier two months early to study French and began classes in September 1988.

Daniel Bourguet taught us Hebrew and Old Testament in ways that made the language and text come alive. He invited students into his passion and curiosity as we pondered both familiar and difficult passages of Scripture. I remember continually being surprised at how seriously Daniel took every textual critical variant, even seemingly irrelevant ones. He masterfully invited and guided us to both scrutinize and contemplate each variant in its original language until we understood the angle from which ancient interpreters had viewed the text. Daniel modeled an honoring of distinct perspectives as we studied the history of interpretation of each passage. He sought to hold diverse perspectives together whenever possible, yet only embraced what the text actually permitted, exemplifying fine-tuned discernment that inspired us.

Daniel's thorough approach meant he would only take us through a chapter or two per semester. This meant we took entire courses on Genesis 1-2:4, on Abraham's call in Genesis 12:1-4, and on Jeremiah 31, Exodus 1-2, Psalms 1-2 and others. In each of his courses he

---

the IPT, writing many high quality books and articles.

included relevant rabbinic exegesis, New Testament use of the Old Testament, and the church fathers' interpretations. Daniel imparted his confidence that God speaks good news now as he accompanied us in our reading, making our hearts burn like those of the disciples on the road to Emmaus—and inspiring us to want to do this with others. In alignment with Vischer and Lys he demonstrated through detailed exegesis of Old Testament texts how God's most total revelation in Jesus both fulfills and explains these Scriptures, making them come alive through the Holy Spirit in our lives and diverse contexts.

While living in France every summer Gracie and I traveled from France to Honduras, spending several weeks sharing our learning with Tierra Nueva's Honduran leadership and leading Bible studies in rural villages before returning back for classes in the fall. We had pursued studies in France with the vision of bringing the best scholarship to the service of the least in a deliberate effort to bridge the divide between the academy and the poor. Our experience of the rare blend of scholarship and pastoral sensitivity, which you will see for yourself in his books, contributed to us feeling called back to the church, into ordained ministry, and back to the United States to teach and minister there. I benefited from his being my dissertation supervisor as I continued to integrate regular study into our ministry of accompanying immigrants and inmates as we launched Tierra Nueva in Washington State.

Daniel Bourguet's writings are like high-quality wine extracted from vineyards planted in challenged soil. Born in 1946 in Aumessas, a small village in the Cévennes region of France, Daniel Bourguet grew up in the heartland of Huguenot Protestantism, which issued from the Reformation in the sixteenth century. He pursued studies of theology at the IPT in Montpellier, including study in Germany, Switzerland, and at the Ecole Biblique in Jerusalem. In lieu of military service, Daniel served as a teacher in Madagascar. He was ordained as a pastor in the Église réformée de France in 1972, serving parishes from 1973 to 1987. Daniel wrote his doctoral dissertation[5] while serving as

---

5. See Daniel Bourguet, *Des métaphores de Jérémie*, Paris : J. Gabalda, 1987.

a full-time parish pastor—a common practice in minority Protestant France, where teaching positions are scarce and pastors are in high demand. This practice often proves fruitful for ordinary Christians and theologians alike, deepening reflection and anchoring theologians in the church and world.

During our residential studies in Montpellier from 1988 to 1991, Gracie and I witnessed Daniel's interest in the early monastics and Fathers of the Eastern church. In 1991 Daniel became prior of La Fraternité Spirituelle des Veilleurs (Spiritual Fraternity of the Watchpersons) and felt called to be a full-time monk, leaving the IPT in 1995 for a year in a Cistercian monastery in Lyon before moving to his current site in Les Cévennes in 1996.

Joy, simplicity, and mercy are the three pillars of Les Veilleurs, an association of laypeople and pastors founded by French Reformed pastor Wilfred Monod in 1923 (with a Francophone membership of 400 in 2013). Members of this fellowship commit to pursuing daily rhythms of prayer and Scripture reading, including noontime recitation of the Beatitudes, Friday meditation on the cross, regular engagement with a faith community on Sundays, and spiritual retreats and reading that benefits from universal devotional and monastic practices. Les Veilleurs has served to nourish renewal in France and influenced the founding of communities such as Taizé. Under Daniel Bourguet's leadership Les Veilleurs thrived. As a member of Les Veilleurs I attended many of his annual retreats, witnessing and experiencing the vitality of this movement firsthand.

Daniel Bourguet's teaching and writing since his departure from his professorship at the IPT in 1995 have focused primarily on equipping ordinary Christians to grow spiritually through engaging in devotional practices such as prayer, Scripture reading, and contemplation. Other works that will hopefully appear in English include reflections on asceticism, silence, daily prayer, and the Trinity. All but three of Daniel's twenty-five or so books are based on his spiritual retreats offered to pastors and retreatants with Les Veilleurs. He has offered

Foreword

retreats to Roman Catholic, Orthodox, and Protestant communities throughout France and Francophone Europe and is widely read and appreciated as a theologian who bridges divergent worlds and nourishes faithful Christian practice in France. Daniel Bourguet made his first and only visit to the United States in 2005, offering a spiritual retreat in Washington State. He accompanied me to Honduras on that same trip just after Hurricane Katrina ravaged the country, teaching Tierra Nueva's leaders and accompanying me as I led Bible studies and ministered in rural communities.

Daniel left his role as prior in 2012 and now continues his daily offices, receives many seekers for personal retreats, and offers occasional retreats where he lives and writes. In alignment with the early monastic commitment to manual labor, Daniel weaves black-and-white wool tapestries of illustrations of biblical stories done by pastor and painter Henri Lindegaard. Daniel's unique contribution includes his Trinitarian approach to biblical interpretation wherein he reads Scripture informed by the early church fathers, with special sensitivity to how texts bear witness directly but also indirectly to Jesus, the Father, and the Holy Spirit.

Daniel Bourguet models an approach to Scripture and spirituality desperately needed in our times. He reads the Bible with great confidence in God's goodness, discovering through careful reading, prayer, and contemplation insights that feed faith and inspire practice. Daniel's deliberate reading in communion with the church fathers brings the wisdom of the ages to nourish the body of Christ today. His tender love for people who come to him for spiritual support, and the larger church and world, inform every page of his writing, inspiring like practice. May you find in this book refreshment, strength, and inspiration for your journey as you are drawn into deeper encounters with God.

Bob Ekblad

Mount Vernon, WA
July 7, 2016

Preface

THIS BOOK REPRISES STUDIES presented in March 1999 at Ecully during a retreat of *La Fraternité spirituelle des Veilleurs*. In retreats, as with preaching, bibliographic references are left to one side; they might have had a place in marginal notes, but I have preferred to keep them to a minimum in order to stay close to the style of a retreat, as if the reader had also been invited to take part in a retreat through this book.

The people present at these retreats were believers, Christians, and the reader will see that my remarks assume this. Nothing has been changed here, so a reader who is not a believer will undoubtedly feel uncomfortable at times; for the host of questions that will arise for such a reader I ask pardon; however, to go on a retreat is to retire from the world for a time to be face-to-face with God, and the teaching at a retreat is a means to that encounter; for this, a person would have to be a believer. You need to know this before starting to read the book; I am speaking here as if at a retreat, to a reader who is a believer.

Finally, again as if on a retreat, I have kept the elements of an oral style. You are addressed here as a "reader friend," in the form of a dialogue, a dialogue which doesn't propose to be more than an overture to the most sublime of dialogues, that with God.

So there we are, my reader friend! May your dialogue with God find something here to nourish it.

Introduction

God has many faces, but they all unite in one, that of Jesus Christ. Both successively and at once, he has the face of a king and a servant, the face of a judge and that of a man condemned, a face of extreme joy and that of unfathomable sadness, the face of a sage and, in our eyes at times, that of a fool . . . the list could be pursued; it is not short. Yes, God has many faces but they all unite in just one, Christ, and he is the revelation of them all.

Among this multiplicity of aspects to God, some may be more or less obscured in our day; we have trouble making out their features; others, by contrast, rather forcibly capture our attention. For example, the face of God as judge is very present with us, so much so that many people eventually push God away, unaware that this aspect of him is softened by others. Part of the general tendency is that the face of God the physician is often left in the shade, and this is a face of great gentleness.

It is this face, that of God our physician, that I would like, reader friend, to recover with you, to ponder its beauty. It is important that we not forget that it is just one of God's faces, but it is a face which is turned towards us today very attentively.

As we take time to ponder the features of God the physician, we will discover little by little the degree to which we are sick. Our focus will therefore come and go between God as our therapist and ourselves in our need, between God bent over us in tender care and ourselves

INTRODUCTION

in our search for healing. Perhaps we will then better understand the eagerness of the crowds of sick who flocked from all parts to Jesus.

Before a judge, we seek to hide our ill deeds, to dissemble; indeed we endeavor to avoid such an encounter through fear of being condemned. By contrast, with a doctor we want our illness exposed; we are eager to bring it before his eyes so that the suffering can come to an end. Where God is concerned, our willingness to engage with him is very variable, according to whether we retain the picture of him as a judge or that of a doctor.

Reader friend, let us pause for a moment to see God drawing near to us as a physician, as our doctor.

— CHAPTER 1 —

God the Physician

THE FACE OF GOD as physician is a profoundly biblical reality; I would like to begin with a review of the theme, investigating the degree to which it is a constant through the Bible.

In church history, the view of God as physician was an approach adhered to particularly by the Greek Fathers. The Latin Fathers, little by little, left it aside, and the result is that today it is being increasingly forgotten; instead, the image of God as judge was emphasized, at times to the point of distortion. This Western tradition is so strong that today, despite its importance, we need to take great pains if we are to recover the biblical revelation of God the physician in its true proportions.

I will therefore rest my case on biblical texts, but if I also mention the Greek Fathers, it is in simple thankfulness since it is they who have helped open my eyes to this aspect of revelation.

Indebted as I am to the Greek Fathers, I am also to Jean-Claude Larchet; he became their spokesman in an enormous book[1] which is also very present in what I will be saying; however, so as not to overburden my remarks, I will not actually be citing it. Where Larchet is almost essentially patristic in his approach, I wish to stay close to the biblical testimony which forms the basis and the support for the Fathers' elaborations.

---

1. Jean-Claude Larchet, *Thérapeutique des maladies spirituelles,* Le Cerf, Paris, 1997.

Spiritual Maladies

One of the major difficulties we will encounter stems from the fact that in the Western world the discourse of psychology has prevailed over the spiritual. Words which are common to the two methodologies have come to be somewhat booby-trapped; they don't have the same resonances, and this leads to misunderstandings. I will be using them according to their spiritual acceptation, whereas they can be all too easily understood according to the psychological; thus, there is ambiguity today if we speak of maladies or sicknesses of the interior life. My intention is to keep to a discussion of spiritual maladies, knowing full well that doubtless others may immediately think in terms of psychological illness; this is to be avoided. Spiritual maladies are those such as pride, avarice, or lust; not schizophrenia, neurosis, or psychosis. Please be careful! There is a wide range of potential misunderstandings.

Our interior life can be understood along two separate lines, the psychological and the spiritual; complicating matters further is that God does not occupy at all a similar role in the two methodologies. In modern psychological discourse God may be taken into account, but is then generally regarded as just one of the possible factors in traumas. In the spiritual discourse, God is ever present; it is he who fills the role of therapist, and, indeed, is seen as the only therapist, encounter with whom is far from traumatizing! In short, we see that to approach God as the physician for our spiritual life goes rather against our normal mind-set; we will press forward nonetheless!

May our proceedings be truly spiritual, which is to say born of and illuminated by the Holy Spirit, without whom we cannot but become enmeshed in misunderstandings! May he guide us now in our quest for God the physician!

What the angel said about the name of Jesus

The idea of God as physician is really neither marginal nor secondary in the Bible and finds a source in one of the key biblical words, *salvation*, and again, in the very name of Jesus. What we are looking at is a major aspect of Christian revelation.

In the Bible, a person's name, a proper name, reveals the essence of the person who bears it; it reveals the deep mystery of the person's identity. The name "Jesus" means "the Lord saves," which is to say, "God saves." This name is a confession of faith in one of the most important activities of God. A person who bears this name is invited to witness through his life to the saving activity of God.

Matthew's Gospel (1:21) teaches us that Jesus' name was proposed to his supposed father by an angel; it was neither Mary nor Joseph who decided to give their son this name, but God himself, who made it known by his messenger. When the angel came to propose the name to Joseph, he gave an explanation at the same time, but with a gloss on the sense which is of great importance. The angel did not say, "You will give him the name of Jesus because God saves . . ." but rather, "*You will give him the name Jesus because he will save*," this "*he*" being a designation of the heralded child. It is this "*he*," this child, who will save, not "God." But rather than leading us to deduce from the angel's words some opposition between the child and God, we must simply understand that there is an equivalence; "this child will save" means indeed "God saves," which comes to saying that this child is God himself, the God who saves.

Here then is a first comment to make on the text in Matthew; the child announced, Jesus, is presented by God's messenger as being God himself. This is astonishing enough in itself, but it is confirmed by the rest of what the angel says. The angel proceeds to add to the verb "save" by saying that "*he will save his people from their sins.*" The only one who can "save from sins," which is to say, is able to pardon sins, is God himself, as is taught in Mark 2:7, and also throughout the Old Testament, where the verb "pardon or forgive," *salah*, has only one subject, God. It is therefore very clear from the message of the angel announcing the child that, as a savior from sins, Jesus is none other than God.

This is the intent of the angel's words about Jesus before his birth.

What Jesus himself said

At one particular moment in his life Jesus gave clear expression to his ministry in a way that forms a commentary of sorts on his name; this is found in John 12:47: "*I am not come to judge the world but to save it.*" Here Jesus is in full accord with the angel; his purpose is solely to save. This is the content of his ministry, the meaning of his existence, of his very being. He bears his name truly. He confirms the saying of the angel and assumes his vocation to save; indeed he confirms the angel's words simply by accepting his role as the subject of the verb "save." Jesus was not content to be a prophet who would announce that "God is coming to save"; he says openly, "I am come to save"! We can understand those who saw this as a blasphemy; nevertheless, Jesus enters into what the angel had spoken of him; this son is God!

"I am come to save"; this comment of Jesus is extensively illustrated by the evangelists who take pleasure in enumerating various saving acts of which he was the author during his life. However Jesus' saving activity is not limited to that time frame. We find in fact that after his death and resurrection, Jesus again uses the verb "save" with future reference; "*He who believes and is baptized shall be saved.*" Jesus says this after his resurrection (Mark 16:16), meaning that his saving activity was not fully accomplished on the cross and that it contains another aspect to be fulfilled later, at his return at the end of time, as other texts tell us (see Matt 24:13).

Salvation before and after the cross

In this way, two important stages in the work of the Savior become apparent, one before his death and resurrection, and the other at the end of time. For the angel, these two stages both belong to the future ("he will save"), but for us today the first is past and the other still future.

In the Gospels the two stages are presented under very specific colors:

- before Easter, Jesus presents himself very much as a savior, but a savior who has nothing of the judge about him. His saving activity is altogether outside the juridical. "*I am not come to judge but to save,*" or again, "*I judge no one*" (John 8.15). Indeed, Jesus did judge no one. We will need to specify the way in which Jesus is savior without being a judge.

- after Easter, Jesus again speaks of his activity as future savior, but now taking on in full his role as judge, as is seen in this parable where he depicts himself actually judging: "*When the Son of man shall come in his glory, in the company of all the angels, then he shall sit upon his throne in glory . . .*" (Matt 25:31–46). The continuation of the text describes a great tribunal, the last judgment. It's in this eschatological, juridical context that we hear, "*he who holds fast to the end shall be saved*" (Matt 24:13), or again, "*he who believes and is baptized shall be saved, but he who believes not shall be condemned*" (Mark 16:16), where the verb "*condemn*" clearly shows that this is judgment.

Certainly, the last judgment has a present aspect, to the extent that it is anticipated by the cross. The "not yet" of the eschatological kingdom is "already here," through the cross in its judgment on sin. Salvation is indeed held in a tension between the already and the not yet, the *already finished of the cross* which assures us of salvation, and the *eschatological not yet* which will fully reveal what is now virtual but nevertheless effective. This tension invites us to the faith of which Mark 16:16 speaks. But is this the whole of Jesus' saving activity? Are his ministry, his identity, his existence, his being itself as expressed in his name, are they limited solely to the realm of judgment or do they indeed go beyond this? We have already approached the answer in the verse that says "*I am not come to judge but to save*"; we need to be very sure about this as it concerns the real identity of Jesus, his true being. These are the stakes!

"*God saves*," "*Jesus saves*"; our modern Western world has concluded in retaining only the juridical side of Jesus activity and has posed the question of salvation in terms that are only concerned with judgment. This outlook imposed itself little by little through the Middle Ages to such a degree that by the time of the Reformation the question of salvation was related solely to judgment. The debate between Catholics and Protestants on salvation was framed from the outset solely within this domain; this limitation has made of the whole question a trap from which we still have difficulty extricating ourselves today. The Gospels have a much larger view of salvation, and it is this we must now examine. We see that the stakes are indeed high. We are concerned with our Western theology, but also with the very person of Jesus and the mystery of his being, as found in his name, "the Lord saves."

The eschatological activity of Jesus is juridical, but if the substance of his saving activity prior to his death and resurrection is not the activity of a judge, we need to know what it is.

The master of the cosmos saves here and now

In the account of the calming of the storm, the disciples, terrified by what they are going through, cry out to Jesus, saying "*save us*" (Matt 8:25). The disciples' cry does not mean, "Save us at the end of time, at the final judgment," or even, "Save us through the cross, on the day of your death!" No indeed, and we know it well! This "save us" is an appeal requiring an immediate reply, on that day, in the midst of the tempest. This was not a matter for tomorrow (the cross) or the day after (the last judgment). It is here and now that salvation needs to be effected, a vital salvation of which Jesus is to be the author, not a salvation pertaining to judgment. The salvation of the disciples in the boat is not the salvation of the court room. The disciples' cry is not addressed to a judge, not even to a physician, but to the master of the elements, the master of the waves and the wind, to the one who saves by delivering from the storm.

This Gospel passage reveals that Jesus justly bears his title (God saves), and that the salvation of which he is the author is not merely judicial. This salvation is disengaged from the tension between already and not yet; it is totally integrated into the concrete present, in the present activity of Jesus in favor of his disciples. It is an immediate salvation, which in no way prevents it from being a salvation by grace; it is by grace, in fact, that the disciples are saved from the tempest and not by their merits. We see that the word "grace," like "save," goes far beyond merely the juridical. "God saves"; Jesus saves from the elements of the cosmos of which he is the master. Jesus removes his gown and bands; he leaves the tribunal and walks through the universe as sovereign.

I don't wish to fully develop here this aspect of the person of Jesus; the idea was to no more than touch on the fact that the identity of Jesus, the mystery revealed in his name, his activity as savior, cannot be confined within a narrowly legal framework; this emerges from his earthly ministry, as he himself said, *"I am not come to judge but to save the world."*

The salvation in view here is no less a salvation by grace, to be received by faith, as a further gospel passage demonstrates. When Jesus walks on the water and Peter ventures out to meet him, after a few steps on the water, Peter begins to sink. Immediately he cries out, *"Lord, save me"* (Matt 14:30). In his cry Peter does nothing more than call out to Jesus by his proper name,[2] turning it into an imperative, *"Lord, save me."* His words go right to the heart of Jesus in the full extent of its mystery; he is not addressing him as a judge or a physician but as the sovereign and master of the universe. Jesus does not reply, "Yes, yes, you will be saved at the end of time," or, "On the cross I will save you." No! Jesus reaches out his hand, and with this action he saves, rescues Peter. This salvation is not juridical, eschatological, or even medical; it is greater still and is realized in the present. It is always a salvation by grace. Jesus accompanies this salvation with a question he asks Peter:

---

2. I.e. Jesus—the Lord saves (Trans.)

"Why did you doubt, man of little faith?" (Matt 14:31); so it is salvation purely by grace, and received in such poverty of faith! Blessed be God because Peter was saved despite the smallness of his faith.

The physician saves here and now

We come now to Jesus the savior in the medical realm, and so to Jesus the physician, the healer.

That Jesus was a healer I do not think requires any demonstration. It is enough to read the Gospel to see that Jesus spent his time caring for and healing a great number of people. This is a constant throughout the four Gospels; none of them makes of Jesus' healing activities a sideline to his ministry; quite the reverse!

In Matthew's Gospel alone we find fourteen passages on healing (8:1–4, 5–13, 14–15, 28–34; 9:1–8, 20–22, 23–26, 27–31, 32–34; 12:9–14, 22; 15:21–28; 17:14–21; 20:29–34); this is a considerable number, greater than any other type of account. Seven more brief mentions should be added, which tell in just a verse or two of Jesus' healing activities (4:23–24; 8:16–17; 9:35; 11:5; 14:34–35; 15:29–30; 21:14), as if it were necessary to keep repeating that Jesus' ministry in its physical dimension cannot be truncated. Further, when Jesus sends his disciples out in mission, he charges them to pursue his ministry, including its healing dimension; *"He gave them power to heal sicknesses"* (Matt 10:1, 8).

According to some modern commentators, Jesus' healing activity was more to the taste of the crowds and the evangelists than it was to Jesus himself! It is clear that the crowds were very desirous of healing and that the evangelists were much struck by this aspect of Jesus' ministry, but to say that Jesus made little of this side of his ministry seems to me to be exaggerated. I cannot believe that Jesus was constrained to play the healer for the crowds despite himself.

For Jesus himself, the healings he works are so important that he advances them to make clear the meaning of his ministry and to reveal his true identity, the profound mystery of his person. Indeed, when John's disciples came on his behalf to ask of Jesus, "*are you the one who is to come?*" claiming signs from him which would demonstrate that he was in fact the Messiah, Jesus' answer is very clear; these are the signs he lists in his reply, "*Go and tell John what you see and hear: the blind see, the lame walk, the lepers are cleansed, the deaf hear, the dead are raised and the good news is announced to the poor*" (Matt 11:4–5). His first point is not the preaching of good news (as the commentators I speak of would perhaps wish), but his role as healer, and this in such an imposing way that he states it in all its facets, citing the blind and the dead, before passing on to the lame, the lepers, and the deaf. This wealth of detail clearly indicates the importance of the healing work in Jesus' eyes. This is more important than the feeding of the crowds, the calming of storms, or walking on water.

In short, Jesus fully assumes the role of healer and places it at the heart of his ministry.

To heal is to save

Among the gospel accounts of healing there is one which clearly reveals how Jesus is the "*God who saves*," how the mystery of his person is tied to the realm of physical healing. The passage is the one which concerns the woman with the hemorrhage (Matt 9:20–22).[3] "*Now there was a woman with a flow of blood for twelve years; she came up behind and touched the hem of his garment, because she said within herself, if I can just touch his clothing I will be* healed. *Jesus turned around and said when he saw her, 'take courage, my daughter, your faith has* healed *you.' And the woman was* healed *from that very hour.*"

---

3. The author cites the French translation by Segond, which stresses the word "heal." (Trans.)

We have emphasized the three uses of the verb "heal." In the Greek, the word used is the verb "to save," the same as we have seen up to this point. It can be translated as "heal" to make the physical sense of the word apparent, and it is this which interests me here and is essential to our purposes. The word "save" also means "heal." Salvation clearly embraces the physical. Jesus the "savior" is therefore, in the same way, the physician. He is the physician by virtue of being the savior.

This physical dimension to salvation in no way negates salvation by grace. The woman here does not put any reliance on her own merits in order to be healed; the process is entirely one of faith, as Jesus himself notes; *"your faith has saved/healed you."* To the woman's faith, Jesus responds with his grace; *"the woman was saved/healed that very hour."*

The woman's salvation is not projected into the *eschaton*.[4] This is not "your faith will save you at the end of time," not even "you will be saved through the cross," but *"your faith has saved you"*; this is a past event, not future. The salvation concerns this woman in the now, as the last phrase of the passage underlines, *"The woman was saved that very hour."*

The woman is saved from her ills, from her sickness, and the great question which will occupy us in what follows is to know what the connection is between sin and sickness; this must be if we wish to approach the text on the basis of the angel's statement that *"he will save his people from their sins."* Certainly, this woman formed an integral part of the company of believing people, the people Jesus came to save.

Firstly physician, then judge

On the basis of the passage we have just looked at and all the other Gospel accounts, we can say the following: in the Gospels, the verb "save" in its juridical sense is always used with regard to the future, in a manner more or less tied to the end of time and the last judgment,

---

[4]. Gk, "the last day" (hence eschatology). (Trans.)

whereas the same verb in its physical usage is always directly related to the present. Where the woman says "I am going to be saved," she is speaking about the future, but a future which is so close that it almost immediately becomes past in the mouth of Jesus; "*your faith has healed you.*" The word "save" in its physical acceptation is never related to the end times. The healing activity of Jesus is in the present and is not eschatological.

What we have just looked at will help us understand the words of Jesus just mentioned, "*I am not come to judge the world but to heal it.*" This would seem to mean, "I am not come now to judge the world since this is reserved for later, for the end; but I am come in the first place and right now to heal the world of all the evil by which it is assailed."

Two images of Christ are clearly apparent here, that of a judge in relation to the end, and that of a physician, which has to do with the present. We are surely concerned with both images, but in ways of varying immediacy, according to whether our concern is directed towards the present or the future.

If you will allow me, I will take this picture to show that the two aspects of Christ also concern us at different levels of our lives. There are two ways to "save" a thief: either to forgive their larceny, or to heal them of their predilection in that direction. The judge may save the thief by overlooking their thefts; the physician will save them by curing them of their kleptomania. Before God, the thief can turn to the judge and address him in prayer, "Have pity on me, Lord, in your mercy, save me; forgive my thieving!" He can also turn to him as physician and say, "Have pity on me, Lord, in your mercy, save me; heal me from my thieving ways!" God is at one and the same time both judge and physician, and he receives both prayers, but we see how the fulfilment of them would be different, how he would touch this man at different levels of his being. The grace of the judge concerns our lives at the level of our acts, our behavior, whereas that of the physician concerns our lives when it comes to what causes our actions, at a much deeper level of our being.

The spiritual depth of physical maladies

To consider Christ as healer, we now examine what sort of maladies he heals.

A reading of the Gospels shows Jesus essentially healing physical afflictions. This is well characterized by the passage where Jesus heals the severed ear of the high priest's servant (Luke 22:51).

Today we often have trouble knowing what to make of these physical healings, and this is quite understandable; it is in great part because our conception of a malady is not that of Jesus' epoch. There is one point here on which we need to pause a while.

In Jesus' time, physical maladies were considered inseparable from the spiritual life. For example, lepers were regarded in their physical affliction as impure spiritually (see Lev 13:8; "the priest shall declare him unclean"). They were not allowed to live among the people (13:45–46) and still less enter the temple (see 2 Chr 29:5). They were not allowed to pray or to participate in any way in the life of the temple. When Jesus spent time on the healing of lepers, it was to reinstate them into the integrity of spiritual life.

In the Bible, sickness is at the same time both physical and spiritual; the two cannot be dissociated because a person in God's eyes is one whole being. Today our outlook is different, such that the intensity of our spiritual life is not reflected in the doctor's report.

In Jesus' time the blind and the lame (the most frequently cited ailments in the Gospel texts on healing) were excluded from the priesthood (Lev 21:17–23), but, according to the Gospels, we see that Jesus considered every disciple a priest, as is demonstrated when he forbade a man from burying his father (Matt 8:22; see Lev 21:11, which forbids a high priest from burying his father or his mother). When Peter's letter says that we are a kingdom of priests (1 Pet 2:9), this fully reflects Jesus' view of his people. To demonstrate this, it was necessary for Jesus to heal the blind and the lame; by these healings Jesus opens the door of the priesthood to everyone and gives each person the possibility of full spiritual life.

Today we are a thousand leagues from all this. I know a lame priest; no one has called his ministry into question because of his infirmity. The same applies to Pastor Roger Chapal, whose blindness has not caused his vocation to be challenged. This would indicate the way we have dissociated the spiritual life from sicknesses and physical handicaps. This is a fact, but for this very reason we have difficulty understanding the gospel accounts in which Jesus is so attentive to physical maladies. His attention has an eminently spiritual import. The attention he lavishes is both physical and spiritual.

Where, in the Bible, sickness is linked to the spiritual life, this allows us to understand why it is associated with sin. Sickness is linked to sin in the spiritual dimension.

It is sin which perturbs the spiritual life, as we well know. For us, this does not translate directly into physical sickness; by contrast, to the extent that the Bible links the physical and the spiritual, it is self-evident that sin, as it upsets and perturbs the spiritual life, will also perturb the physical life, and that is what a sickness is, a perturbation, a disturbance of the spiritual life. In short, in the Bible, sin and sickness are linked; sickness is sinful; sickness stems from sin and manifests it.

We know the story of the leper Naaman, healed of his leprosy by the prophet Elisha (2 Kgs 5), and how Gehazi, Elisha's servant, set about extracting, which is to say, stealing, money from Naaman; in a moment of time, the thief became leprous and the leprosy revealed his sin.

We might consider the case of Gehazi a little more deeply and see that his physical sickness reveals his spiritual sickness: the thoughtless love of money.

When the Philistines of Asdod had taken the ark of the covenant (1 Sam 5), they were struck by a violent outbreak of hemorrhoids. For us today, it is most surprising to see this collective sickness placed in relation to the seizure of the ark; in the biblical period there was nothing surprising about it; the sickness was nothing other than the result and manifestation of a grave fault, the theft of the ark of God.

The same sickness is not always found in relation to the same sin. We have seen Gehazi rendered leprous as a result of his love of money. Miriam, Moses' sister, also became a leper (Num 12:10), but for a completely different reason, that of judging and slandering her brother. The same sickness, but different sins; this shows that a person who becomes sick will be aware of their sinful state, but may not inevitably know which of their sins is the origin of the sickness.

Love of money and slander are both spiritual maladies. The two spiritual maladies translated into the same physical malady. Discernment is required to fix on which spiritual malady is implicated in which physical malady.

This then was the situation in Israel at the time of Jesus; a spiritual malady might bring in its train a physical malady, which is its symptom. What would Jesus' attitude be, faced with this?

Jesus and spiritual maladies

Jesus took full account of the mentality of his times, as particular passages show clearly. For example, when the four men carried the paralytic on a stretcher, made a hole in the roof, and lowered him down to Jesus' feet, Jesus speaks in the first place of the sick man's sins; then, faced with the reaction of those around he asks the following question: *"What should I say to the sick man, 'your sins are forgiven you,' or rather, 'take up your bed and walk?'"* Which is to say, should I heal him of his spiritual sickness or of the physical? Then, to demonstrate that he had authority on the spiritual plane, Jesus speaks to the man on the physical plane, *"Take up your bed and walk"* (Mark 2:1–12). Nothing could be clearer; Jesus is aware of the close connection between the physical and the spiritual, but his reflex response is to draw attention to the spiritual; *"My son, your sins are forgiven you."* The physical healing then attests, in the eyes of all, to the re-establishment in its integrity of his spiritual life. This is the same as with the lepers, the blind, and the lame; through physical healing Jesus aims at the reinstatement of the spiritual life. He puts the man back in God's hands, and it is this above all that counts.

In the case of the man born blind in John 9, the disciples immediately ask, as soon as they see the man, what sin it was that caused the physical infirmity; they were truly representative of their time (John 9:2). They were unable to discern the hidden ill, and were counting on Jesus' discernment. It is interesting to note that Jesus put the question of sin to one side(9:3); he simply healed the infirmity. By contrast, the account as a whole is built in such as way as to show Jesus drawing attention to another kind of malady, not the physical but the spiritual. The account closes with Jesus making it plain that there exists a spiritual blindness (9:40–41), the gravity of which is much greater than physical lack of sight.

In Jesus' teaching, spiritual blindness is a theme which often recurs (see Matt 6:22–23; 15:14; 23:16, 17, 26 . . .). For Jesus, this blindness is to be seen in close relation to sin, just as had been stated long before by the prophet Isaiah (Isa 6:10). Jesus makes use of the prophet's phraseology to underline how, while the people's physical eyes were well, they were spiritually blind (Matt 13:13, 15), a sign of their sin; *"they see without seeing, and they hear without hearing."*

In short, in the Gospels, the accent is always displaced from the physical malady to the spiritual; the true handicap in the relationship with God is not the physical but the spiritual malady. Certainly Jesus heals the physical, but his attention is much more drawn towards the spiritual, which he discerns, diagnoses, and wishes to heal in order to re-establish each one into the full integrity of his life with God.

I believe that we do well today to not always consider a physical malady as a spiritual handicap; the spiritual life of someone physically unwell might be as beautiful and rich as someone who is quite well. However, we risk rejecting the Gospel teaching if we are not awake to spiritual maladies, which vitally affect the life with God.

Jesus heals sins

Jesus takes account of the connection between sin and spiritual sickness, but in such a way that he corrects the way sin is regarded. Effectively, the link between sin and spiritual sickness means that Jesus looks at sin less in its penal aspect and more as something to be cured. He does not judge the sinner; on the contrary he labors to treat and heal him.

When the Evangelists cite Isaiah 6:10, it is very interesting to note that the people who are sick with sin are converted so as to be "forgiven" according to Mark 4:12, or to be "healed" according to Matthew 13:15 (see also John 12:40; Acts 28:27). Mark here keeps sin in the penal sphere, whereas Matthew, Luke, and John place it in the medical. This hesitation of the Evangelists about the verse from Isaiah show that sin pertains thoroughly and simultaneously to both the penal and the medical. However, all things considered, Jesus himself seems to have considered sin more from the medical angle than the juridical; it is rather as from the mouth of a healer that we should understand the statement that *"I am not come to judge but to heal."*

This outlook of Jesus on sin modifies our outlook on sin. Before a judge, I hide my ills, my sin; before a physician I expose it. So, according to the way Jesus invites me to look at my sin I will either hide from God or open up to him . . . what a turning point in the spiritual life with the discovery that Jesus presents himself, above all, as a physician!

God heals sins

To think of sin in its remedial dimension is not an invention of Jesus. The Old Testament very often envisaged sin from this angle. For example, when there is a question of the infidelity of the people of Israel, in a context which threatens condemnation, God suddenly changes his tone and speaks in this way to the people, *"Return and I will heal your unfaithfulness*" (Jer 3:22). God does not speak of "pardoning" the unfaithfulness but of healing it. God presents himself not as a judge who is merciful, but as the physician to the people's sins, the healer of the spiritual malady of unfaithfulness.

Earlier, before Jeremiah, God had said the same thing in the mouth of the prophet Hosea, "*I will heal their apostasy*" (14:4).

God heals every disease

That God might be a physician is no surprise to anyone in Israel. Not only, in fact, does the Old Testament consider God to be a physician but regards him as the only one. In the Old Testament, the verb "heal" has God as its only real and effective subject (Gen 20:17; Deut 32:39; 2 Kgs 20:5 . . .) Human medical practitioners are sent by God, unless they are charlatans (Hos 5:13). It is only with God's help that a doctor can heal the sick, and if he doesn't have God's help, he will be exposed to rejection by, and mockery from, God (Jer 8:22).

The sicknesses which God treats are physical ones to be sure, but not these alone. The psalmist says it well; "*God heals you of all your diseases*" (Ps 103:3). To whom is the psalmist speaking here? To his own soul! He is therefore speaking of the infirmities of his soul, and it is these which are the spiritual maladies. "My soul, God heals you of all your diseases." The psalmist speaks here of "all" the diseases of the soul. This is to say that God is both the general and specialist physician of all spiritual diseases, without exception.

If God is such a physician, it is no wonder to find the psalmist addressing him in the following terms, "*O Lord, heal my soul!*" (Ps 41:5). God is indeed the one to turn to in order to expose what is wrong. Quite equally, it is towards Christ, himself God, to whom we can turn, to say to him, with the psalmist, "Lord, heal my soul!"

God is the only true physician, just as he alone is judge, the only one who can "heal," as he alone can "pardon."[5] To heal and to forgive sins belongs to God alone, whether the sin is to be seen as concerning the judge or the physician, the courtroom or the hospital! This double dimension of sin appears in the Bible from the first occasion God encounters it. This is very clear, but our Western outlook is so clouded by the juridical that we tend only to see one aspect of things. Let me explain!

When God says to the man he has just created, *"You shall not eat of the tree of the knowledge of good and evil because the day you eat of it you will die"* (Gen 2:17), what is God's role at this moment? "That of a judge!" say all the Western commentators, without any further question. The judge warns Adam of the sanction that threatens him should he ever break the commandment; and, indeed, God himself will put the sanction into effect. The death announced is of a penal nature; it is a condemnation.

This is one, limited reading of the text; things can appear in another light, that retained by Eastern commentators, following the Fathers. Adam is being warned more by a physician than a judge. This physician puts the man on his guard against a poisonous food so toxic that it is fatal. The warning goes like this; "Attention, don't eat this plant, because it is like a death-cap toadstool; if you eat it you will die the same day!" Death is presented here, not as a sanction inflicted by a judge, but as the consequence of an imprudence, vigorously warned against by the physician. It is the ingested plant that brings with it death; it is the plant that kills, not God. Such is the warning, full of love on the part of a physician solicitous of his patient's life.

What happens when Adam eats the forbidden fruit? What is his reaction? He seeks to hide himself from God; he seeks to hide his wrongdoing, which is to say he sees God as a judge. Adam hides far from the judge instead of throwing himself on the physician to implore his aid; "Quick! I ate this fruit; heal me before I die!" Adam's reflex

---

5. (See above "The physician saves here and now.")

action is just like ours. He has of God just the one picture, that of judge. Why? Because the serpent has intruded upon his mind, presenting God as a rival, jealous of his prerogatives. In presenting God this way, the serpent depicts him as someone who will condemn a presumptive rival rather than heal him.

The serpent was the one who initiated sin; his goal was to alienate from God. His venom impels us to hide from God, rather than throwing ourselves into his arms. Another power is needed, another force which will impel sinful humanity towards God, the power of the Holy Spirit; he it is who turns us towards God, and who teaches us to pray like the psalmist, "*Lord, heal me!*"

The serpent alienates sinful humanity from God. Jesus opens the door to the Holy Spirit, who prods the sinner in the direction of God. The serpent depicts God as a judge who is ready to condemn. Jesus opens our eyes to the forgotten face of God, the face of the healer. Jesus restates what the prophet Isaiah had already said, "*I will heal them*" (Matt 13:15, from the Greek text of Isaiah).

Jesus too heals all sicknesses

"*Bless the Lord, O my soul! Who heals all your diseases*," says Psalm 103, representing to the soul the healer of all its spiritual ills. "*He heals you from every disease.*" This last expression, strictly reserved for God, is applied in a very significant way by Matthew to Jesus at the moment he presents him for the first time as healer; "*healing every disease*" (4:23). Matthew insists on this, repeating the expression in 9:35, to show indeed that, in Jesus, the healing God of the Old Testament is made manifest, the one who heals all diseases including the spiritual. When Jesus appears as judge, it is at the end of time. Meanwhile, he is the physician, unceasingly. "*He went through all Galilee, teaching in their synagogues and healing every sickness and every disease among the people. His fame went out throughout Syria and they brought him all those who were suffering, taken by all sorts of sicknesses and torments; the demonized, lunatics, the paralyzed; and he healed them*" (Matt 4:23–24).

The healing disciples

Then, when Jesus defines the role of the disciples and their task on earth, he forbade them most severely from judging (Matt 7:1). If the disciples, alongside Jesus, will one day function as judges, it is at the end of time, like him; "*You will judge the twelve tribes of Israel*" (Matt 19:28). Meanwhile, for the immediate present, Jesus gives them power to heal sicknesses, indeed "all" sicknesses (Matt 10:1), thereby associating the disciples with his healing ministry, including the realm of spiritual sicknesses.

Thus associated with the ministry of Jesus, it becomes urgent that we learn more about the spiritual ills, maladies. If this is our calling today then we are doubly implicated; in so far as we are the sick, since these spiritual maladies are ours too, and then also, as healers who are associated with Jesus' ministry.

The task before us is immense. If we are to be healers, it must be as servants of the one true healer, which means that we begin by refocusing the eyes of all on this healing face of God. To begin here is a substantial task, to such a degree has the West obscured God's role as healer, emphasizing his role as judge.

Everything says the same today, and you know it as well as me; for our contemporaries, before anything else, and almost solely, God is a judge; one whose time is spent condemning, or should the case prove better, forgiving; but always as a judge.

The healing aspect of confession

What is there of all this in the practice of confession? It matters little whether this takes place in the confessional, or in the office of a priest or pastor, it is generally the antechamber to some place of judgment where whatever it is that brings the threat of a penalty is exposed to a person of law; not as in the waiting room of a hospital, where whatever is in need of care is exposed to the healer. It is forgiveness which is sought, not healing!

To be sure, forgiveness is important, but healing is too. Forgiveness is for the wrong of which I am author; healing is for the wrong of which I am a victim or the wrong to which I have been exposed by my imprudence. The two must not be confused! We speak about the "cure of the soul" in Protestantism, as pertaining to healing, but we actually live it as though it were penal. We speak of the mercy accorded us by the judge, but never speak of the care lavished upon us by the healer, whether preventively or as a cure. The cure of the soul is what it is; the opening of the heart to God, in the immense hope that he will know how to care, bandage, heal, and guard against relapse . . .

The healing aspect of the Law

This alteration to our outlook and discourse about God will also extend to changing the way we think about the Law (the Torah, the law of God). Quite obviously the Law has to do with the juridical, but we shrink and atrophy it if this is all we see. The Law also pertains to the healing area, but this is forgotten to such a degree that it requires just about a conversion of mentality on our part. Everything I have said about Genesis 2:17 can be said about each of God's commandments.

The Law of God is also a prescription given by a physician. As well as being a legal code, the tables of the Law are an ordinance prescribed by the physician to those who wish to keep their good health or to recover it.

More than an order, the Law is an ordinance!⁶ Let me explain.

The healing dimension of the Law belongs solely to Israel. Indeed, Israel was entirely innovative in this area, thus separating themselves from the neighboring peoples who constructed legal codes which were purely juridical. I am pausing a little on this point because it seems so essential because of all the misunderstandings about biblical Law.

Among the peoples neighboring Israel, all the law codes present articles of a casuistic nature; "If someone does such and such, this is how they are to be sanctioned." On this point, Israel follows its neighbors; but alongside this, Israel is quite distinct, bringing in another type of article, termed the apodictic. It is truly an innovation. Right up to the present day, to my knowledge, no other law code contains apodictic articles. What are these?

They are found, for example, in the Ten Commandments. *"You shall not make any graven image," "Remember the day of rest," "You shall not murder," "You shall not steal"* . . . these instructions have the peculiarity of not being followed by any sanction. There is no sanction or penalty in view; that is to say, there is no indication given of there being a judge who will intervene in case of disobedience. In fact, these articles have no reference to any judge.

"You shall love your neighbor as yourself" (Lev 19:18); this commandment is an article of the Law; it is apodictic; it has nothing to do with any judge. What in fact would a judge do if presented with someone who had not loved his neighbor as himself? Nothing! He can't intervene; it is not within his competence. He lacks the second item of the article stating the penalty, which is necessary if a judge is to dispense justice.

The apodictic articles do not come from the pen of a jurist but from that of a physician who is giving an ordinance, enumerating the various prescriptions to be respected in order to live in good health.

6. Or prescription. (Trans.)

"Remember the day of rest," "You shall not commit adultery," "You shall love your neighbor as yourself"... It is an ordinance either for cure or prevention, according to the case.

You see the nature of the Law of God; for sure it has juridical elements (in the casuistic articles), but also, indeed, above all, there is a healing dimension (in the apodictic articles). The Law is thus the way to good spiritual health. It serves both to reveal the extent of sin, and through this, to diagnose the seriousness of spiritual maladies; it also serves as a prescription to follow in order to recover good health; it marks out the route to good spiritual health.

Good news, God is our physician

It is a matter of urgency today to reiterate to our contemporaries that God is a physician. "Brothers and sisters, rejoice! God is our healer!"

It is a matter of urgency to tell this to all those who are suffering from their sins in the same way we suffer from a sickness. We must not be content to remove blame from people; this is not enough. Removal of the sense of blame is not always enough to cause an exit from the realm of the juridical; it is also necessary to treat people for their spiritual maladies. To remove blame for their larceny from a thief does not heal them of their thieving, and the same applies to all spiritual maladies.

It is a matter of urgency to tell this to those who rush to psychotherapists, there to expose their ills, but also to seriously risk not hearing the word of God who heals. *"Just speak a word and my servant will be healed,"* it was said to Jesus (Matt 8:8). If the psychotherapist does not feel authorized to speak this word, who will do so? It is because of ecclesiastics declining their vocation as healers and thereby doing away with the healing words of God that the sick have deserted the confessional for the sofas of psychotherapists.

It is even a matter of urgency to sieve through our translations of the Bible, still so marked as they are by Western legalism. I am still flabbergasted by, for example, Segond's[7] translation of Jeremiah 3:22, "*I will pardon your infidelities,*" when the intent is "*I will heal your infidelities*"!

It is a matter of urgency to recover the therapeutic dimension of salvation, the healing dimension of life with God. The Greek Fathers guarded all this and the Eastern church, following their lead, has maintained this fullness of spiritual life. Thus, when an Orthodox goes to confess, the process leads them to Christ the physician, to whom they says, like the psalmist, "Lord, heal me."

The Orthodox period of Lent is a time of repentance introduced by a most beautiful text from St. Andrew of Crete (sixth century), which prompts a turning to God the physician, imploring the grace that heals; "Here I am, covered with sores; my heart devoured by the fever of sin; O true physician, the one whom you love is sick; Lord, if you wish, you can heal me." To go through Lent like this fully opens the heart to God, not in fear of judgment, but athirst for healing.

The atrophy of our theology

Luther was quite right to speak of humanity as being at once both sinner and justified; it remains that this be completed by speaking of humanity also as at once both sinner and healed.

What does this contraction of Western theology to the juridical, as evident in Catholicism as Protestantism, stem from? No doubt there are a range of reasons the full extent of which escapes me, but among them I am aware of two, as follows.

First of all, we need to recognize that the Latin[8] genius is very juridical, so it is not surprising that this should have marked Western

---

7. Important French translation from the early twentieth century. (Trans.)
8. The reference here is to the ancient Roman legal system. (Trans.)

theology. Then, by ill fortune, Calvin was a jurist, and this has not helped bring resolution to the dialogue with Catholicism, which has eventuated in an impasse.

Then Paul himself, the holy apostle, profoundly contributed to Western Christianity by limiting itself to the juridical, and we know the importance that Paul's letters have had in the development of Western theology.

In the Apostle's writings, for example, the verb "save" (*sozein*) is never used in its healing context, the inverse of the gospels. Therefore if a theology of salvation is built only on Paul's writings, it will perforce entirely lack the healing dimension, otherwise so present in the life and message of Jesus.

The verb "treat, tend" (*therapeuin*) is not used once by the Apostle Paul, although we are well aware from the book of Acts that he cared for and healed a great number of people! (see 16:18; 19:11–12; 28:9). In his writings, Paul never spoke of his healing ministry, which was nonetheless very active.

The verb "heal" (*iasthai*) and the word "sickness" (*nosos*) are likewise absent from Paul's letters.

In short, this omission of important words from the healing vocabulary has certainly contributed to the way the west has had little openness to this dimension of theology and spiritual life. By balancing the teaching of Paul with the contents of the Gospels we can, I believe, restore to theology its full scope and recover the face of God as physician, one of the faces of the God who heals.

— CHAPTER 2 —

A Divine Consultation

GOD, THEN, IS A physician, the only physician who really knows how to heal the most recondite places of the soul. It would be a good idea if we could now pass in review the different maladies of the spiritual life, but there are so many that it is not possible to examine them all in this little book. Rather than launch into a superficial enumeration of them, my preference is to stop on just one and see, on the basis of one biblical text, how God acts in his role as physician towards a person touched by this particular affliction. In some sort, we will be onlookers at a consultation.

The account of a consultation I have chosen is found in the Old Testament. I prefer this to a Gospel text in order to show that already in the Old Testament, God is a healer.

I had the choice of many texts; my preference is to dwell on one which distinctly concerns a spiritual malady, without any possible confusion with something psychological. A spiritual malady separates from God whereas a psychological one does not. Schizophrenia does not separate from God any more than does the chickenpox, whereas pride, avarice, or anger all do.

The spiritual malady we will look at is anger. It appears in the first pages of the Bible and concerns us all to a greater or lesser extent, without our necessarily having ever really gauged its gravity. The passage is that which describes the first known case of this malady, that of Cain.

A Divine Consultation

Here is the passage from Genesis 4.[1]

1. Adam knew Eve, his wife; she conceived and gave birth to a child, Cain, and she said: I have formed a man with the help of the Eternal. 2. She gave birth again to his brother, Abel.

Abel was a shepherd and Cain worked the land. 3. After a certain period of time, Cain made to the Eternal an offering of the fruits of the earth; 4. and Abel, for his part, made the offering of one of the firstborn of his flock and of its fat. The Eternal looked favorably on Abel and his offering; 5. but he did not look favorably on Cain or his offering.

Cain was very angry and his face was downcast. 6. And the Eternal said to Cain: Why are you angry and why is your face downcast? 7. Certainly, if you do well, you will lift up your face, and if you do ill, sin lies at the door,[2] and its desires are directed towards you: but you, you must rule over it.

8. Then, Cain spoke to his brother Abel; but, as they were in the fields, Cain threw himself on his brother Abel and killed him. 9. The Eternal said to Cain: Where is your brother Abel? He replied: I don't know; am I the keeper of my brother? 10. And God said: What have you done? The voice of your brother's blood cries out from the earth and reaches me. 11. Now you will be cursed of the earth which has opened its mouth to receive from your hand your brother's blood. 12. When you cultivate the ground it will no longer yield you its riches. You will be a wanderer and a vagabond on the earth.

13. Cain said to the Eternal: My chastisement is too great for me to bear. 14. Here you are chasing me today from this land; I will be hidden far from your face, I will be a wanderer and a vagabond on the earth, and whoever finds me will kill me. 15. The Eternal said to him: If anyone kills Cain, Cain will be avenged sevenfold. And the Eternal placed a sign on Cain so that whoever found him would never kill him. 16. Then, Cain distanced himself from the face of the Eternal, and lived in the land of Nod, to the east of Eden.

---

1. The French gives the translation of Segond, which is here rendered into English. (Trans.)

2. KJV nicely says "crouches" at the door, but see below. (Trans.)

I don't intend to dwell on anything in this text except as it concerns anger. There are other possible approaches to the passage, but I am putting them to the side.

The way I shall proceed will be influenced by the Fathers, which requires of us a certain amount of effort today, but I shall do everything possible to facilitate entrance into this way of doing things.

The Greek Fathers have the enormous advantage of forming a single school in their approach to spiritual maladies. This unity is very stimulating for us when compared with the rifts to be seen today in the therapeutic schools of our Western world. Furthermore, the school of the Fathers already has more than fifteen hundred, if not nearly two thousand years of experience, which is enormous compared to what can be cited for the modern schools.

It is therefore in the lineage of the Fathers that I position myself; this needs to be known if I am to be understood, though it is a tradition to which you are in no way obliged to adhere. That at least is my position and, in my eyes, it is what gives the best account of the biblical teaching. You will do with it as you please, but I believe it is worth the effort to attempt to tune in to this way of thinking.

I am going to do no more than report what the Fathers have said. My only original contribution will be to make constant reference to the Hebrew text, which the Fathers did not do; they all worked with the Greek text (or the Latin), which sometimes departs from the Hebrew.

We now set to on this text from Genesis. Since we are limiting ourselves to what concerns anger, we turn directly to what is mentioned in verse 5.

Cain was very angry

This is the most common translation; it is very much an approximation and requires us to pause. I actually find it rather unsatisfactory, but recognize that it is difficult to accurately convey the Hebrew.

A Divine Consultation

For us, "Cain" is the subject of the clause *"Cain was very angry."* In the Hebrew expression it reads differently. "Cain" is not the subject, which is to say that Cain does not take the initiative in becoming angry. This is very important. We never actually deliberately set about becoming angry. We do not say, "Hah! I'm going to become angry now!" No! Anger comes along of itself.

In Hebrew, the subject of the expression which concerns us is impersonal. We could translate it something like this; "This was very irritating to Cain." In this expression it is as if the true subject wishes to be hidden, beyond reach. In short, Cain is not the subject, which is to say that what takes place in him does not proceed from him. "This inflamed Cain greatly" is another way we could translate it; "this" inflames him, "this" angers him, "this" produces these states in him and Cain finds himself with an accomplished fact, with a situation that he must cope with, either by dominating or allowing himself to be dominated by something bigger than he is, something he has not yet learned to contain, and of whose origin he is ignorant.

In fact, if we take an overview of the biblical usage of the verb used here, we see that its subject is not as indeterminate as this; in reality it is implied. Nevertheless, I am speaking of it here as indeterminate because this is certainly the first use of the expression in the Bible, and, more, it describes something that is happening for the first time in Cain's experience, and indeed in the history of humankind. We need to go further in our reading of the Bible to find named what is passed over here in silence. Poor Cain! Nobody could tell him that "the thing that inflamed him" means "anger inflamed him."

The understood subject here is indeed the word "anger." In fact, of the eighty-one uses of the verb in this form (the qal form of *harah*), twenty-six of them are impersonal like this. In fifty-four other passages, the subject is always the same—"anger." This is indeed the word that needs to be understood here: "it, anger, was very hot in what concerns Cain."

It is clear, then, that anger was at work in Cain, but the word *anger* does not appear in the passage. Anger was working without showing itself to Cain, who therefore, inevitably, has difficulty identifying it in order to take note of and fight it. He needs help or advice from someone more aware than himself.

Something else which is important to note is that in the Bible no person, any more than Cain, is ever the subject of this verb, which surely shows that a person never decides to become angry. One time alone (and this is the final passage, of which I have not yet spoken) the subject of the verb is God himself (Hab 3.8)! This is most astonishing! "God inflames himself with anger." To designate God as the subject is no doubt a way of indicating, in my view, that God is not subject to anger, he is not the victim of it as are we, but is its master. God can intend to be angry while maintaining sovereign control over the anger, and he is indeed the only one to have such mastery. It is most important to recognize this difference between men and God when it comes to anger, in particular as we continue with Cain's story.

The Master of anger here draws near to someone discovering anger in themselves for the first time and being unable even to identify it. God will draw near to Cain and speak to him as to a friend, as an expert, to help him out of his evil situation.

He does the same for us. Anger always arrives brutally; it grabs hold of us in a hidden way, without naming itself. If we don't think of turning to God, it is he who approaches us, as we will see him do with Cain.

Anger

In Hebrew the word for "anger" (*'ap*) also means "nose," indicating that the nose is generally where the intrusion of anger can be seen. An angry person's nose changes appearance; it gets red! That is to say, anger is manifest physically by different symptoms; a reddening of the nose and face, by trembling, by stammering, by bulging eyes . . . and the Hebrew fixes on one of these symptoms in its term for anger.

"Anger," "nose"; this also means that internal trouble has physical repercussions, showing how in the Hebrew everything is linked. The human person is a whole; the physical, the psyche, the spiritual together form a unified whole.

"Anger," "the nose"; one might say that anger is seen as a central feature like the nose in the face! Indeed, just like the nose, it is visible to others but not to the subject, who is unable to hide it while it is hidden from him or herself!

In the suggestion of the nose becoming inflamed, it's clear that this is a fact related to healing rather than justice. A judge has nothing to do with inflammation of the nose! Quite the reverse, a doctor will regard it as a symptom which will help in diagnosis. Here, it is a symptom of anger. The expression we are studying describes a sudden crisis which assails Cain; "this was very inflammatory for him."

He was *very* angry

If there is inflammation, this is very important; it means the crisis is acute and in fact, we realize as we examine the rest of the Bible, speaks of the most acute state of anger. Nobody indeed is ever "very, very" angry; the worst attacked are "very" angry (Gen 34:7; Num 11:10; 16:15 . . .).

In short, the very first crisis to affect Cain is immediately of the most serious nature. The Fathers noted the differing degrees of anger and took efforts to detail them, from a simple bad mood all the way to fury, passing through animosity, bitterness, belligerence . . . When they speak of "anger" this is a generic term covering all the shades of this spiritual malady.

The Fathers also noted that the word *anger* may serve to designate something other than a malady; it also indicates "righteous anger" or "holy anger," the anger which does not separate from God but, on the contrary, animates the spiritual fight against all that could separate us from him. This holy anger is also that of God as he fights against all that separates a person from themselves.

Cain

We said with regard to Jesus that a name reveals the identity of a person, the mystery of their being. What of Cain? It is an interesting name.

First of all, it was given to Cain by his mother, who explains the choice making a play on words with the verb *qânâh*, which means "acquire" or "procreate."[3] "*I have formed a man with the Lord*," as our translation says. Eve affirms here that God is a father to Cain, and indeed God behaves as a thoroughly admirable father throughout this passage. The spiritual father is certainly more of a physician to the soul than he is a judge. It is with both the love of a father and the abilities of a physician that God sits down at the bedside of his sick son.

But also, the name Cain makes a play with the verb *qana*, which means "*to be jealous, full of zeal, ardent,*" and this makes Cain the prototype of the passionate and fervent; for this reason, when the Fathers comment that anger is a sickness of the passions, it means that Cain is engaged, assailed in the depths of his being, at the core of his identity.

For the Fathers, the soul comprehends three functions: passion, desire, and reason. Passion, like the other functions of the soul, is positive, created by God. A person is in the image of God and this with regard to passion as well. God himself is passionate, zealous, jealous, except that he does not become sick in his passions in the way people do.

In his passion, in his jealous zeal, God turns against everything that can assail humanity, his covenant partner. In the same way, a

---

3. The KJV perhaps tries to recreate this—"I have gotten a man from the Lord." (Trans.)

person's passion turns against everything that might assail his covenant relation with God. This passion that protects the covenant relation with God is a passion of great good, but a person's passion can easily be led astray and become sick. This is the case when it mistakes its goal and seeks to protect other bonds, other attachments. Passion falls ill when it throws away its concern for the divine connection in favor of alternatives. Anger is surely a spiritual malady since it affects relationship both with God and one's neighbor.

Cain, passionate, full of zeal and jealous, in the image of his spiritual father, here becomes sick in the depths of his being.

His face fell

The word *face* is always plural in Hebrew because it is considered as representing the different features: the nose, the eyes, the ears, the cheeks. A face is seen as multiple in its composition and also in its expressions. Here the features of Cain's face fall; they are distorted. This is a description of the physical, the exterior and visible; the expression describes a change in the features as an external symptom of internal trouble, a troubled passion, a trouble deep within Cain. The external symptom will help the physician in his diagnosis of the internal problem, the malady affecting Cain.

His features fall, are distorted; Cain no longer seems himself, and neither does he resemble his father. He is not in the image of God. The real Cain is passionate, zealous, but not angry. The sudden access of anger makes Cain hardly recognizable; an angry person indeed does not seem him or herself; they are not themselves. The image of God is distorted, as are the features of the face.

The Eternal said to Cain

This is incredible! The angry Cain is yet to make a further move; he neither hides himself nor throws himself on God. He has not so much as opened his mouth, and yet God intervenes without waiting, as quickly as possible, more quickly than a rocket and before Cain manages to pick up the phone!

What will the intervention be? That of a judge? But Cain has done nothing, said nothing that would justify such an intervention. He is quite simply angry.

By contrast, the intervention of a physician is fully justified. Cain is suddenly and profoundly sick. Indeed, it is a physician who comes to speak to Cain, and much more—it is his spiritual father.

Why are you angry and why is your face fallen?

In fact, God asks not just one question but two. Perhaps he even left a pause between them, expecting a reply. Cain responds to neither.

Would a judge ask such questions? Certainly not! A judge asks about actions, and Cain has done nothing. It is not even he who has intended his anger, but anger which has taken hold of him. "*Why has this inflamed you so?*" asks God. The truth is that Cain here is more a victim of anger than the guilty party. We know that Cain will later turn murderer, but at a present he has not raised so much as his little finger. No, a judge has no reason to step in here.

It is rather the physician who sits down at Cain's bedside to ask his patient about the changes in his appearance: "why this reddening of the nose and why this downcast look on your face?"

God thus begins his consultation, asking questions about the symptoms he notes so as to reach a diagnosis with a view to prescribing an appropriate treatment.

Why?

When God asks questions like this, it is not that he doesn't know the answers. God, in fact, sounds out the kidneys and the heart[4] and so understands the symptoms in the nose or the face without having to ask questions! When he asks, the objective is more that Cain will ask too, ask himself the questions, "Why am I angry and why are my features downcast?" The spiritual father is a good teacher!

God does not ask about the strength of the anger ("*Why are you very angry?*"), but the reason which has given birth to the anger; "for what reason are you angry?" We see that God is guiding Cain to look within himself, to take a good look at his behavior and the hidden motivations behind his state of mind. God is helping Cain realize what has provoked his anger; he reveals to Cain that anger comes in reaction to something that provokes it. This truly is a spiritual father helping his son to discern things; the questions are positive, friendly, and salutary.

All this is most just; anger is provoked by some fact, but we don't always know what; or alternatively, we don't want to know. Meanwhile, to discern the cause of the anger, to look it in the face, is to already be on the road to healing. God is seeking with these questions to set Cain in this direction.

What then is the fact that has provoked Cain's anger? This is told us in the previous sentence of our passage; it is the fact that God has accepted Abel's offering but not Cain's.

We might think that it is Abel who has provoked Cain's anger by making an offering at the same time. Cain had indeed taken an initiative that Abel immediately followed, but, if that were the reason for Cain's anger, he would have become angry earlier. His anger would have been signaled immediately after the mention of Abel's offering, even before God responds to the two offerings.

No, it is not Abel but God himself who has aroused Cain's anger!

---

4. See Psalm 26:2. (Trans.)

God knows why he accepted one offering rather than the other, but Cain knows nothing. God does not explain himself, but here he asks Cain in order to find out how he felt about and understood this choice. "*Why are you angry?*" also means "How has your understanding of my attitude produced such a state?"

Cain, however, has no desire to reply! This silence is embarrassing. Faced with Cain's silence, the Fathers have sought the answer to God's question, and we shall try as well.

I don't believe that Cain's anger proceeds from the fact that God prefers mutton to fruit or even shepherds to growers. Rather, I believe God chose the second offering rather than the first because it is that of the younger brother, not the elder. It is Cain alone who took the initiative in making the offering, an excellent initiative which speaks of Cain's love for God. God has not required any offering, so Cain's is freely given; it is the gesture of a freely given love. Abel has done nothing but copy! The initiative belongs to Cain, to the elder. God should have honored this initiative, honored the right of the elder brother, honored this act of love.

Cain was attached to his initiative, to his act of love, to his rights as the elder. I would say right here that passion becomes anger when it protects something to which it is more attached than God or neighbor. So, Cain is attached to the fact that he is the older brother and the initiative he has taken. When God doesn't honor this, he undermines this attachment of Cain's; he undermines Cain's self-love. God's choice has wounded Cain in his self-love and the anger betrays this wound. This is very common; anger bespeaks a wound to self-love.

This is something anger can signify, what it might translate into, but it doesn't state or formulate it. Now it is Cain's place to do just this, to find a way to put it into words before God. But he is silent!

Why should we seek to reply in Cain's place? It's because through this text God is searching us out too, about our anger. "Daniel, why are you angry?" Faced with a question like this, I am going to have to learn how to answer. This is why the Fathers sought to see clearly what it is that provokes anger. When a physician questions, it is good to know how to respond; it is part of the healing.

By digging into the reasons for anger, the Fathers perceived that wounding of self-love can bring to light various spiritual maladies.

Cain might have been attached to his rights as the older brother in the same way one can be attached to some item as a piece of personal property; in this case his attachment would be a form of the spiritual malady known as avarice; avaricious of his right to seniority.

Cain might have found in his seniority a reason for pride, another spiritual malady; a Cain attached to his rank would be wounded in his pride.

He might also have been frustrated not to have been honored by God as he expected. In this case he would be attached to others' opinion of himself, which is another form of spiritual malady, vain glory.

As we see, the same anger might be the expression of pride, avarice, or vain glory, as well as other latent ills, buried but revealed by the anger which is their symptom. We also note that it is easy enough to discern the anger, but that to discern the malady behind the anger is more difficult.

When we come down to it, the question posed by God is essential, welcome, and even salutary; it is an invitation to discern the deep-seated ill hidden behind the anger. God asks the question precisely because there are a variety of possible answers. He is thus an excellent spiritual father, an excellent doctor to the soul—two facts joined at the hip.

It is now for Cain to say whether he finds himself to be proud, avaricious, attached to vain glory, jealous, or something else . . . but his reply is awaited!

The account is wonderful, leading us to the discovery of a multitude of points noted by the Fathers. In particular this: one spiritual malady often hides another; it is its symptom, because it comes wrapped in it, as if it were its daughter. What we have noted about anger is of value when it comes to other spiritual maladies in that each can be a symptom of another. In such a case, the spiritual malady should no longer be treated as though it were the sickness itself, but as a symptom of something more profound, something it manifests and which should be the real object of treatment. Just as there are connections between spiritual maladies and physical maladies, so there are connections between different spiritual maladies.

By taking a contrary position we can see how anger could be the symptom of another, more hidden malady.

If Cain was not proprietorial, avaricious of his position as the elder, he would not have become angry, but would rather rejoice to see himself dispossessed of his asset in favor of his younger brother.

If Cain was humble, he would marvel to see God exalting the lesser.

If Cain was not attached to vainglory, he would rejoice to see the honor God has done to Abel.

All this clearly shows, it seems to me, that behind Cain's anger another spiritual malady is hiding.

If then a malady can be symptomatic of another malady more deeply buried, the Fathers would apply themselves to the treatment of the hidden malady rather than the symptom. One can well understand that in the healing of the buried malady, the symptom will go, whereas healing of the symptom will not cause the deeper sickness to leave. In short, to heal anger, it is the hidden malady which must be treated.

Further though, since the maladies hidden behind the anger vary with each case, we understand why the Fathers propose different remedies for different cases of anger. For example, anger could be treated by fasting if the anger comes from an excessive attachment to food ("greed"). It could be treated by charitable giving if the anger proceeds from avarice, etc. All this is correct; avarice healed does not become angry when its money is touched; the healed gourmand does not become angry when wronged with regard to food. This would also suggest that it is not easy to treat oneself; there must be discernment of what lies buried within.

A Divine Consultation

Without the help of a physician of the soul, who are we to discern what is hidden? In general, it is only after many fits of anger that we can work out in ourselves what the source is; it is usually for the same reason that we become angry, not for other reasons, so, when the same situation repeats itself, we do eventually learn. With the access of anger, we note the source; I leave you to examine yourself. But here, what about poor Cain?! This is his very first crisis of anger! Happily for him, it is God himself who questions him in order to help. If Cain's responses to the physician are not clear, this itself will push him to be more precise, to the point where he can see the source of his anger.

But he doesn't reply!

Cain's silence is understandable; the one who is questioning him is the very cause of his anger. The physician is himself responsible for the crisis he wishes to treat. It is he who has made the patient sick! The consultation has reached an impasse.

This is what so often happens; we wish to be treated by God, but it's God's fault that we are sick, or so at least we think . . .

Nevertheless God draws near. God takes the first step; he could do no more. In effect, he comes to reconcile things and with his question he holds out the olive branch to Cain, for him to vent his spleen, his bile, his anger on God. God knows that Cain is angry with him, and he comes to reconcile. This is the best remedy that God can offer Cain for his healing. "*Why are you angry?*" God awaits an answer something like, "It's your fault! You shouldn't have looked down on my offering . . ."

However, Cain does not answer! The drama of anger is that it sometimes refuses reconciliation; the anger then closes over once more on the wrong done it, and becomes resentful in its silence.

God's attitude in this process of reconciliation is very important for us. God humbly takes the first step towards us and offers us his hand. The response he awaits is prayer. Prayer is a remedy for anger. To pour out one's anger before God is a wonderful remedy, even if it is anger directed at God. The physician is quite used to being attacked by the patient; he is used to the pus when he lances an abscess. Even if Cain feels the need to curse, God is ready to listen to the cursings of his prayer if this will be liberating for him. He doesn't come to judge but to heal.

Prayer comes from a heart that is opening; this opening up is essential in any therapeutic process, and this is what God is awaiting, looking for, and what he wishes to provoke with his questions: the opening up of our heart before him.

If it is difficult for us to discern the reason for our sicknesses, here too, in prayer, we can ask God for insight. To tell God that we lack discernment is also prayer; it is once more to open our heart to him.

When Cain begins to open his heart to God, he will have taken the first step along the road to healing. Instead, Cain obstinately refuses to go down that road.

Faced with this silence, there is no capitulation from God. He perseveres in his approach, as do the best of spiritual fathers, the best doctors of the soul. He doesn't leave Cain to enclose himself in silence.

"If you do well . . . if you do ill . . ."

What God says is perfectly clear on one point, that Cain has not yet sinned. Thus, we are absolutely not dealing with a judge; it is not a judge speaking to Cain here but a physician.

The physician here informs Cain of possible developments to the situation according to the attitude he, the patient, chooses to adopt. God sheds light on a possible quick recovery (if you do well, your countenance will be lifted), or serious complications (if you do ill . . .). It all depends on Cain.

Anger is not a sin; it is the first stage in a process that may become sin, but there is no necessity to this. Opening up of one's heart does not necessarily mean confession of sins; it may be anterior and precede sin;

and its object may be to avoid sin. Opening one's heart to a spiritual father is not confession to a confessor.

At this moment Cain has undergone an access of anger; anger has inflamed him. Now God shows him that it is up to him, Cain, to step in, that he is at a crossroads and that he can intervene in the progress of the anger; "if you do well . . . if you do ill," this is the crossroads.

What God says is quite indeterminate, but I believe this is deliberate on his part. From the outset, Cain has said nothing. God is just looking for the one thing, that Cain speak, that he enter into dialogue. When God is so imprecise he wishes to provoke Cain to speech, to ask the questions we would all have on our lips; "but Lord, what does doing well consist of? What does it mean to do ill?"

But Cain still says nothing!

Faced with this silence, the Fathers have investigated what positive action Cain might have taken to put a stop to the anger, and what positive actions we can take as remedies for anger. We have seen that the remedies vary according to the malady the anger is masking, but leaving this aside, the Fathers have noted by experience the remedies able to heal any anger. Two of these are love and humility; acts of love, undertaken in humility, heal every kind of anger. This is certainly true; bear it in mind the next time you have a crisis of anger and you will see how the anger loses its grip.

Self-control is also a remedy for anger as you will no doubt realize, but you also know that it can be extremely difficult to control oneself when angry, more difficult indeed than in other situations. The stronger the anger, the more difficult it is.

Love, humility, self-control . . . all of them come from God; each is given when we ask. It is precisely the case that God is present, awaiting some word from his patient, some prayer; he is there, ready to give the remedy we ask of him. In some sort, God is both physician and pharmacist! Therefore we have a double need of him if we are to be healed!

Among the remedies for anger, there is another the Fathers noted without knowing it had perhaps been suggested to Cain by God himself. A knowledge of Hebrew is needed to see this; the Greek translation of the passage misses it.

After the phrase, "if you do well," there is a difficult Hebrew word commonly translated as "your countenance will be lifted," but which can quite possibly be translated as "forgive!" If there is anything to this, then God is showing Cain the way; "if you do wish to do well, forgive!" Forgiveness; what a wonderful remedy for anger. If you are angry, forgive the one you think is responsible for it . . . This indeed is what Paul says to the Ephesians: *"Bitterness, irritation, anger . . . all this must depart from among you. . . . Forgive one another mutually"* (Eph 4:31–32).

If you do ill, sin is crouching at the door

This phrase imparts an altogether remarkable teaching on sin. God speaks here of sin lying in wait at the door of Cain's house, which is to say outside, external; this means that Cain has yet to have dealings with it. To be angry is not a sin. Anger may eventuate in sin, but there is no necessity for it. This indicates a certain interval between the present situation, which requires a physician (the onset of the fit of anger), and what eventuates, which requires the judge (sin). The physician comes before the judge, and indeed we discover that God the physician appears first and does all he can to prevent the need for intervention as a judge.

Sin is outside Cain, but at the same time is directly linked to Cain's attitude: "if you do ill." This expression is a way of speaking of sin, now presenting Cain as the responsible party; from this angle, sin proceeds from Cain. "If you do ill" means "if you sin." How right this is, that sin comes from both outside a person and from within; a person is both responsible for and a victim of sin.

In saying that sin comes from within a person, we must make careful distinctions. In effect, sin comes from the "doing ill," while our passage clearly shows that, if Cain does ill, he does so under pressure from anger; he is a victim of anger, a person who is sick, and not one who is bad in himself. The evil action does not spring from a Cain who is bad, but from a Cain who is sick, and we have seen that the sickness comes from outside Cain and not from Cain himself ("anger inflamed Cain"). The evil action comes from Cain in so far as anger is working on him.

All this is to say that a person does not emerge bad, a sinner from the hands of the Creator. A person in themselves is good. They are even "very good" according to God himself (Gen 1.31). Nevertheless, this good being can fall sick and, under the influence of the sickness, can act badly and thus sin. In so far as they are sick, they need God the physician, a God who will step in quickly to prevent them turning aside to sin; then they would stand in need of God the judge.

Sin is crouching at the door

This expression presents us with a personification of sin. This is most interesting since it puts sin in the role of the instigator of sin, not the sinner. The sinner will indeed prove to be Cain, not the one who is lying at the door; but sin will be the fruit of the encounter between the instigator of sin and the sinner himself. This is the same process as in the account of the serpent in Genesis 3; the serpent is the instigator of sin and sin is the result of the encounter between the serpent and Eve.

The verb "crouch" used here is one which is used to describe animal behavior. Sin is thus presented rather in the guise of an animal than a person. The verb can be used of a person, but in these cases it is always to liken the person to an animal (Gen 49:9, 14, where Judas crouches as a lion, and Issachar like a donkey).

The animals that crouch in this way are very diverse so that it is not possible to know to what animal sin is here likened, but it is not a serpent; the serpent is never the subject of this verb, simply, no doubt because a serpent is already lying down! It would never be adopting this position, crouching down!

In the rest of the Bible, the animals which are subjects of this verb are: the sheep (Gen 29:2), the lion (Gen 49:9), the donkey (Gen 49:14), the panther (Isa 11:6), the calf and the bear cub (Isa 11:7), the crocodile (Ezek 29:3), and even the demons (Isa 13:21), which shows that the Bible classes the demons with the animals, or compares them with animals.

Cain then is warned that an animal is crouching behind his door, but he doesn't know if he has to do with a sheep or a panther! Nevertheless, if God is urging him to master it, the animal must be dangerous, an adversary, but one a person can control.

God's warning is of great interest; it allows Cain to accurately identify his enemy and thus not to mistake it, which is again a marvelous gift of God to this angry man. As you know, an angry person is no longer able to correctly identify his friends and his enemies; this is true to such a degree that they are liable to attack innocents. An angry person's reason is distorted; they look everywhere for an adversary on whom they can vent their rage and may well get it wrong.

God takes good care of Cain and points out to him where he should unload his anger; not on the innocent Abel but on the beast behind the door. Abel is not Cain's enemy and neither is God. On the contrary, he has a real enemy, sin.

Among the animals enumerated in the Bible, we have seen a place for the demons, and this, finally, is where the Fathers have settled their focus in speaking of sins, or rather of the instigators of sins.

At the door

What would the door be other than the door to the heart? This is how the Fathers understood it and I would find it difficult to see things otherwise. We thus, surely, retain the image of Cain on the inside and the demon on the outside. God is warning Cain of something he is unaware of and can't see. This is a beautiful picture which speaks to us of the reality: God reveals to us the presence of the one we cannot see at the door of our heart, that is, sin or its instigator.

Evil is outside of us, like an animal crouched at the threshold of a door. If it comes inside it is because we have opened the door of our heart to it; but at first it is outside, which surely means that, by nature, a person is good before they become a sinner. The Fathers are perfectly biblical on this point; humanity, created in the image of God, is good. The tragedy is that a person opens the door to anyone who happens along, even after God's warning.

At the very moment God is cautioning Cain that a beast awaits him behind the door, God himself is on the inside, speaking with him. He is a wonderful spiritual father! It is a miracle of God that he has this place in our heart, closer than the closest of friends, to care for us, to teach and illumine in order to keep us from sin. There is no one closer to us than God, present in our heart in a way which is so thoughtful and loving.

Even better, God is present when our heart is sick. Cain's anger has not caused God to flee; on the contrary, it has caused the physician to call, for the very reason that Cain is sick with anger. No; Jesus said, I am not come for those who are well! I am come for the sick! It is a fact that God leaves Abel to the contemplation of his offering and comes to care for Cain; he leaves Abel in his good health and visits Cain in his suffering; he hasn't spoken once to Abel, but comes for a lengthy discussion with Cain! He comes to save the one who is sick and may perhaps sin. God has no repugnance about approaching sick hearts but cares for them diligently, with a Father's love.

In his dialogue with Cain, God is for now the only one to speak; he questions and advises, just waiting for the one thing, that Cain speak too, that he answer the questions, that he react and express his feelings. This is what God is waiting for from every sick heart—a word; that's what prayer is, a word addressed to God, whatever may be said.

When you are unwell, pray, open your heart to God. The reality is that God has already entered your heart; I don't know how, but he has already come in without being horrified by whatever he discovers of unhappiness or suffering. He has entered in order to awaken prayer within you, to bring it to birth. He is in no hurry. He is there to help with his solicitude, his listening, just like a father bent over his sick child.

Why then should we attach such importance to what Cain will say to God? Because the one behind the door will hear what Cain says as well! This is an essential point, a great spiritual truth noted by the Fathers. The evil one listens behind the door of our heart. If he hears us speak with God, converse with him in prayer, he understands that we are on God's side and he gives up; he retreats, sooner or later. In contrast, if he only hears God speaking, he takes note of our refusal to pray, rejoices and stays by the door. He knows that we are closed off to God and that we will soon open the door to the outside in order to get away from him. That is the one thing he is waiting for; he knows that he has every chance if we shut ourselves away from God.

So when you are sick, pray. When you open up to God you are keeping the door of the heart shut to evil. Pray then, and the evil one will quit . . . I promise you; it's true! Prayer causes the wicked one to despair!

A final remark about the door to the heart is that the demon is outside, and God is within and Cain too; Cain is at home; it is his house. If anyone opens the door it will be Cain and no one else. The beast outside has no way to open doors! Our resistance to evil, in this sense, is tremendous; Cain is under no obligation to open, but can stay safely within, with God; this would be best thing for him to do, particularly in his state. Once Cain begins to speak to God, he will calm down; an angry person will eventually calm down once they begin to speak. God is patient, more so than the beast; he will wait as long as is needed.

The demon connected to the anger is no more patient than the anger, which becomes inflamed and burns like straw, violently but quickly. This particular demon always winds up quitting, well before God! If you are angry, be patient and you will quickly be healed. Be patient, just as God is; indeed ask God for patience; his pharmacy is well-stocked and everything is free. He will know how to supply the remedy if you ask it of him. Patience—another cure for anger!

Patience will enable the fire of anger to be extinguished, but there is another attitude in which to stay home; Cain can stay home and entertain the fire; he can stubbornly entertain the anger, declining to unclench his teeth and unwind before God. Then, though the demon of anger is not so patient, if he quits it will be to fetch his daughter, bitterness, who can stay a step from the door for years and years, even for an entire lifetime. Be on your guard; in your obstinate exclusion of God, bitterness[5] will take anger's place!

Bitterness is a malady which takes longer to heal, but it is not incurable. The unanswerable remedy with which to rid yourself of it is prescribed by God himself: *"you shall not bear a grudge against any of the children of your people; thus, you shall love your neighbor as yourself"* (Lev 19:18). Indeed, love for one's neighbor cures bitterness. Therefore, Cain, Abel is your neighbor, so rejoice in his joy, and bitterness will not come near.

Alongside love is found forgiveness, another particularly effective remedy. Bitterness, indeed, has no idea about forgiveness and so melts before it like wax in fire. Bitterness has anger as its mother and pride as its father; it receives its aversion to forgiveness from its father.

If you remain obdurate in your stubbornness, bitterness will soon go looking for its daughter, sadness, and she too will come to settle

---

5. Literally, rancor or spitefulness.(Trans.)

down at your door. If you persist, sadness will call her daughter, depression, who will also take up residence; and so your countenance will never cease to be downcast. I am telling you that you had better go and rejoice with your brother. If you do not make friends with obstinacy towards God, the beast that attacks your heart will quickly decamp.

Its desire is toward you

The word used here for *desire* designates amorous desire, whether the love of a man for a woman (Song 7:11) or of a woman for a man (Gen 3:16). Here, we are dealing with the lustful desire of an animal for a man, which is to say a desire which is contrary to nature. An animal which becomes amorous towards a man; here is a way to say unequivocally that sin is against nature! It is as much contrary to nature as a block of wood in the eye. A person is born naturally good; they might be born with some congenital deformity but certainly not with a lump of wood in their eye!

The second thing this word from God teaches us is just as important; what it reveals about sin is fundamental. The image of an animal crouched at the door might lead us to think of an animal on the watch, ready to spring on its victim; but that is not it. The animal lying there is doing so voluptuously, lustfully. This indeed is its whole mode of deception; the demon is ready not to attack but to seduce. This is certainly what happened with Eve; she was not so much attacked by the serpent as seduced. The important thing to know is this; sin lusts after us! It is a perverse lust, contrary to nature!

But Cain has a wonderful God and spiritual father, who helps Cain defend himself against the evil before it has even begun its game of seduction. Indeed, it is not the wish of the evil one so much to devour us as to possess us; it devours us in the possessing. As we become attracted to our evil, to our sin, we become possessed by it. A great deal of spiritual lucidity is required to uncover the lustful relationship we entertain with our sin, but God does give us this lucidity; he opens our eyes. We know how an alcoholic suffers from his poison, but also how he loves it. The same with the gourmand. A person overcome by lust enjoys his fall. An angry person manages to find a certain delight in their anger. A proud person is far from being discontented in their pride . . . all these spiritual maladies are against nature but they install themselves in the homes of their lovers as if they were their own. For this reason the Fathers call them "passions" rather than sins. A passion is a sickness that installs itself over a long period of time to the point of becoming a person's second nature. The word *passion* is well chosen; it speaks both of suffering (as in the Passion of Christ) and of the intensity of an amorous relationship (to love with passion). Such, then, is the beast which lies at our door: a passion.

But you, you must rule over it

The verb form used in the Hebrew is not the imperative but indicates something which is not yet complete, as in "you will finally rule over it." The sense is that of an imperative, but it is more the command of confidence or of a promise. God speaks with a tone of confidence; "I know that you will rule over it; I have confidence in you about this; I know you well enough to know that you can do it." The note of promise is there too; "Don't be afraid, you will overcome it!"

There is nothing better God could say to Cain. What else could he say? He is a good father who knows how to express all his love and confidence, and is well able to communicate his expectations.

The use of the verb *rule* shows that God considers Cain a competent adult. Only adults are the subject of this verb and it is a catastrophe if a child begins to govern (Isa 3:4). Even when sick, Cain is an adult, able to rule over the one who wishes to seduce him.

In speaking like this to Cain, God is also appealing to the nature expressed by his name; is he not zealous and fervent, someone who can give of his best to dominate his own hot-headedness? Fervency is what is needed to fight against sin, against the one who seeks to separate humanity from God. Go ahead, Cain; you are the exemplar of fervency. Anger has not weakened this ardor; stir it up! You will dominate all the more easily while sin is vulnerable, lying voluptuously in front of the door!

The whole of the spiritual fight is here, not with the brother, not with God, not with oneself, but with the seducer, the instigator of the sin. The battle may be fierce, drawn out, and perhaps even seem unequal but God says "do not be afraid, you will rule over it."

In the clash of strength which spiritual combat presents, we may well ask what sin's strength is, the strength of the seducer, the strength of the demon, the strength of the beast lying at the door of our heart. It's power is very strange, and here again the Fathers are inspired observers. The beast's strength is whatever it can draw from us! It is a veritable leech that draws strength from its victim. In itself, sin's only power is that of seduction. Once it has seduced us, sin senses our complicity and sucks from us the strength our complicity gives. The more it installs itself, the stronger it gets; the longer we wait, the more it strengthens itself and the more our strength to fight fails. But it is also enough to refuse it just once and it begins to lose its strength. If you resist the evil which has taken hold, the first fight will be hard, the second easier, the third still more so because you have ceased to feed it with your complicity; it loses the strength you refuse to give it.

On the other hand, what of a person's strength against their adversary? Their resources are those which God gives them and which he gives liberally to those who ask. The resources to fight the passions lie in the fruit of the Spirit: love, patience, self-control, gentleness—these resources move mountains!

If Cain had asked God, "How can I rule over it?" God would have replied: "With me! Remember, Cain, what your mother said when you were born—I have formed a man with the help of the Eternal! It is so true what she said; your life is with me; your natural fervency comes from me; your domination of sin will also be with my help. As your name is, so is your life. Without you, sin has no strength; it finds its strength in you. You yourself have little strength, but in me there is no lack. Go ahead, Cain, now; you can open the door to confront sin and if you ask, I will go out with you."

Cain spoke to his brother Abel (1)

It is extraordinary but Cain says nothing to God, not a word! Cain's silence before God is truly tragic, a tragedy for both Cain and for God. It equates to the closure of the heart to God, and the fact of closing the heart to God is the opening of the door to sin; the two cannot be separated. This is what Cain does; he closes his heart to God and by this fact opens the door to the demon. We know the result: the demon has won.

What is the reason for the silence? We should ask the question if we wish to understand ourselves better.

I believe it lies in the way Cain fails to see God as a friend, but rather sees him as the source of his anger, and that just because God's idea of justice is not the same as his. Cain's system says that God should honor the first offering, that of the elder. The justice of God is to honor the younger, the weak (Abel's name speaks of his evanescence: steam, breath). God's justice means inviting the strong to rejoice that God's favor is fixed on the weak to lift him up.

Cain's silence might have still other reasons. It could be that Cain didn't really hear all that God came to tell him. This would not be so surprising; anger can indeed make us hard of hearing. When you have spoken to someone who is angry you are sure to have noted that they don't listen. Anger prevents us from understanding others, as well as God. While this may be true, it is so only in part.

When Cain fails to respond it could also perhaps be that he is wounded in his heart, believing God's love for him to be lacking. God's gesture of love towards Abel could be understood as a lack of love for him. If God loves Abel, it means he loves Cain less, or not at all! This is a point of view which fails to realize that God's love has no measure, that it is beyond measure for both Abel and Cain. A person gives their love by measure and believes that God does the same. Here is why Cain might be shutting God out in silence: spite! Wounded in his heart, Cain is therefore affected in his desires, this other faculty of the soul, alongside his zeal. We see that the anger first of all affects his innermost passion but then next affects his desires, like a gangrene that spreads.

Desire, passion,[6] and reason; these are the three faculties of the soul. Anger stems from the inner passion, wins over the desires, and then spreads further to the reason. Cain well knows that his anger comes from the position God has taken and that Abel is innocent; nevertheless, it is not God he intends to grab but Abel! The gangrene of anger settles in and spreads. Who would say that anger is not a serious spiritual malady?

The other symptom which shows the seriousness of Cain's condition is his silence before God. We observe that throughout his fit of anger Cain says nothing to God; his dialogue with God is nonexistent, his relationship with God is nil, and his life with God is dead. God may speak to him but he does not reply. He doesn't listen. God finds himself alone, talking to himself. God is present in front of Cain, but Cain is not there with him. All this is because of anger; the presence of the anger suppresses the presence of God; it kills his relationship with God before it kills the brother. When the anger has disappeared, Cain will recover dialogue with God; he will recover life with God.

---

6. Desire here would mean what a person wants, whereas passion (zeal) speaks of a burning inner motivation. (Trans.)

Cain spoke to his brother Abel (2)

This is a translation which completely ignores a difficulty. The Hebrew simply says, "Cain said to his brother Abel"; the difficulty is not in the words as such but in the fact that Cain says nothing to Abel! We wait for remarks which never come! We could, like Chouraqui,[7] add some dots: "*Cain said to his brother Abel . . .*" The Greek resolves the difficulty by filling the gap ("let us go out into the field"), but I prefer to stick with the Hebrew.

Something very important becomes apparent in this truncated account. We see Cain refusing to dialogue with God, and he instead precipitates a discussion with Abel. He rejects the dialogue initiated by God, and himself initiates another. Then the dialogue he starts is itself cut short, so short indeed as to be aborted before it begins, given that we don't even know what Cain said. We don't know so much as the first word. This dialogue is more than silent—it doesn't exist!

Does Cain at least know what he said to his brother? Surely not! Anger does not know what it is saying; this is one of its characteristics. It is a gangrene that affects the reason.

Would Abel have replied? Whether he did or not, it would only have fed Cain's anger. To reply to an angry person inflames the anger; not to reply inflames it as well!

The truncated Hebrew account is amazingly true to life!

Cain threw himself on his brother and killed him

The anger begins to exteriorize itself in the aborted words before it moves on to action. This is the classic process. An angry person begins by letting loose the heat of his sickness in meaningless but forceful words, then in actions which are more violent, before reaching an extreme of violence, just as happens here. The progress into violence has

---

7. A recent French translation. (Trans.)

its origin in Cain's passion, which is then heated by the anger to the point of becoming murderous. With the murder the anger is assuaged, as if sin, the seducer, had engaged sexually with Cain: an excitation leading to a paroxysm, and then, when the anger is gone, satisfied, Cain is left exhausted and alone.

To combat this escalation, the indispensable remedy was surely self-control, which would have checked the process. To control one's actions is very difficult for an angry person; the best way is first to gain mastery over one's words, before the anger becomes too strong. Before even that, Cain could have taken control of his thoughts, because this is the place where we permit or do not permit the beast at the door of the heart to enter; the door is our thinking. Mastery of thoughts—this is where God intervenes, at the level of the heart, at the point when self-mastery is easiest. But Cain did not wish this; he opens his heart to the beast, and it is the beast which masters Cain; it masters his heart, then his mouth, and then his hands.

Self-control is one of the gifts of the Holy Spirit (Gal 5:22–23), so we know to which pharmacy to repair to find our remedy.

Cain has not mastered his anger but allows himself to be mastered by it. The murder is perhaps an uncontrolled act; if it is controlled, it is not by Cain but by the anger. Anger makes Cain do whatever it wishes, even something Cain, doubtless, does not wish. Cain becomes possessed by anger, by this demon.

Anger has mastered Cain's passions, for sure, because this is what it works on first, but it also gains the mastery over Cain's desires and reason, taking total control of his soul. Cain's desires are thoroughly dominated. Desire, in fact, is the source of love and we see Cain here kill brotherly love. Cain's reason is also dominated in that he kills an innocent person! This is not logical, but it is the logic of anger.

When Cain became angry, we have seen that this might have stemmed from his being wounded in his self-love as the elder son, and that the anger was born of this wound. Perhaps in what followed, when he spoke to Abel, Cain initially did little more than cry out with the cry of wounded self-love, but then anger impelled him to turn murderer. A murder for a wound, what a crazy exchange; but such is the lack of proportion in anger, its form of logic. Wounded self-love murders brotherly love!

Certainly Cain kills Abel who is innocent, but in fact the guilty party so far as Cain is concerned is God; but even by anger's logic you can't kill God, so, unable to do that, Cain grabs hold of Abel; he grabs God's witness, the one on whom God's favor has alighted. This too is classic; when we can't take hold of God, we grab his servant, his witness (in Greek the word for "witness" is *martyr*). Christ is prefigured here, announced in the martyrdom of Abel. Given that we cannot kill the Father, we crucify the Son; we kill the one God loves; this is the logic of the beast at the door.

In Cain's view, if God preferred Abel's sacrifice to his own, it is apparent that God loves Abel and not him. Wounded in his self-love, Cain seeks to wound God through his love for Abel. The angry person, wounded by God, attempts to make God angry. This is a sort of provocation, a challenge to single combat in which one wishes to fight with God as with an equal! Pride establishes itself in the wake of anger; love for God gives way to hatred of him. This again is the logic of the beast which lies voluptuously at the door of the heart.

The crisis of anger has passed, ending in a crime. The anger is dissipated in the shedding of blood. We could finish our reading of the text at this point, given that our attention is focused on anger as a malady to be treated by a physician. Now that Cain has become a murderer, it is time for justice. It is God's place to intervene in his capacity as judge, and no longer as a physician.

But it is good to continue reading all the same, particularly to observe the behavior of an angry person after the crisis of anger and how God will respond to the excesses of anger; will it be as judge or physician?

The Eternal said to Cain: where is your brother Abel? He replied: I don't know _____

Finally (but is it not too late?), a dialogue opens between God and Cain, a real dialogue this time, in which Cain responds to God's questioning, no longer a dialogue of the deaf. We see that the anger is passed; Cain has recovered his hearing!

Where is your brother Abel? _____

God knows very well where Abel is! He knows where he is, right before his eyes, lying still unburied in the corner of a field. He knows very well because the cry of Abel's blood has filled his ears. The question God asks is not designed to uncover some piece of missing information, but to finally open a discussion with Cain, the discussion he has not yet managed to have. God here pursues his profound desire, to converse with Cain.

But who is it who wishes to engage in this conversation, the judge or the physician? No doubt both of them, it seems to me.

"*Where is your brother Abel?*" This question might be that of a judge to someone who still has blood on their hands, but it could also be that of a physician who is moved to care for his patient after their crisis of anger; it is this physician who particularly interests me here.

Anger can be treated before, during, and even after a crisis; this is something we need to know! God does not renounce his care for his patient; he might now sink into despair when he sees the irreversible nature of what he has done, and believe that his present state is irreversible too. Will this anger prove to be a chronic sickness? We can ask and find out!

"*Where is your brother Abel?*" By speaking the word "brother" and using the name of Abel, God acts as a true spiritual father who still seeks the opening of his son's heart. He investigates the fraternal relationship, the brotherly love; by so doing, he seeks to show Cain the road to repentance; "*speak to me about your brother*"! By this question, God shows that he is waiting on Cain for his repentance.

Repentance, this is the remedy, the best of remedies after a bout of anger, however violent. It's a remedy which prevents irreversible loss of hope.

Repentance is a remedy because it revives love and is a step of humility, and this in turn engenders gentleness; gentleness is the healing for anger. Gentleness prevents anger from becoming established in a chronic way; it is the recovery of good health.

Certainly, when it comes to judgment, Cain has no way out from the murder, but God opens a door to him, that of repentance. The judge opens the door of repentance to bring him pardon and favor. God, in fact, is a judge who is "*merciful, slow to anger and full of love, who forgives . . .*" (Exod 34:6–7). Cain had perhaps endeavored to provoke God to anger, but at each turn he encounters not anger but the love which opens to him the door of repentance: "*Where is your brother Abel?*" This door opens upon the way of forgiveness, the way of healing.

I don't know!

Instead of opening his heart, Cain closes it, and closes it with a lie. Cain pursues his logic, or rather the logic of the beast which separates from God. Silence was the closing of the heart; the lie locks it. After killing his love for his brother, Cain shuts the door on repentance and kills his love for God.

Am I my brother's keeper?

It might be believable that with this "*I don't know,*" Cain is telling the truth. Some angry people might indeed not know what they are doing in their outburst of rage. We say of them that they recover their reason which they had lost. But with the question that Cain now asks God, the lie becomes clear. Cain, in fact, is the elder brother and is well aware that, as the elder, he is indeed his brother's keeper. Cain restates his rights of seniority. He had become angry because this right was not respected. He knows better than anyone that he is his brother's keeper, and the falsehood of his lie comes to the surface with this question: am I my brother's keeper?

The voice of the blood of your brother cries out

"*God said: what have you done? The voice of the blood of your brother cries out from the earth and reaches me.*" The murderer's lie has no weight compared to the cry of the victim. It is the judge who now steps in, to bring the murderer to a confession. There is nothing more for the physician to do. The spiritual father does not force a door which is shut and locked . . .

Unless . . .

You will be cursed

"*Now, you will be cursed of the earth which has opened its mouth to receive from your hand the blood of your brother. When you till the soil it will not give you its bounty. You will be a wanderer and vagrant on the earth.*" Such is the sanction of the judge; it is not a condemnation to death for murder; Cain receives a punishment which is certainly rather merciful. The earth will no longer give him as a laborer what he needs for food or for offerings to God. As a laborer, he will have to wander the earth as a nomad, or perhaps like a shepherd, with or without a flock, in place of the shepherd he murdered . . . But his life is saved.

My punishment is too great to bear

"*Cain said to the Eternal: my chastisement is too great to bear.*" God's sentence on Cain has a surprising effect, altogether unexpected for us, but, no doubt, not unexpected by God. Cain finally says something true, and he says it to God! A true word and a real dialogue; Cain finally opens his heart. A miracle! This is what God had awaited, what the spiritual father looked for.

What happened?

Quite simply, the judge's sentence has brought about the opening of the sick person's heart. The physician can now heal his patient. Opening the heart is the route to healing because the physician can enter the heart and tend it. This is fine discernment on the part of a spiritual father who knows how to provoke the heart to open and how to bring forth a true word and a real dialogue. Truth is the road to healing.

This moment in the account makes it apparent that God, by his shrewd intervention, is at once both judge and physician and that he well knows how to reconcile the two; in this he is a true spiritual father. Here the judge's sentence is a healing act with a salutary effect.

In thinking about what we see in the Bible and in our lives, I believe we can indeed generalize here. God is a judge whose every sanction has a therapeutic value and content; each sanction has the effect of a remedy with draws the evil out of one's heart. This is how we are to reconcile the two roles of God and avoid seeing them as opposed. We consider the judge, and marvel to see in him a physician. We consider the physician, knowing that at times he can adopt the attitude of a judge to arrive at his goal, to save people. This is the Savior God, the "God who saves," Jesus.

The Western church has failed in its task, by speaking only of God's justice; but it can also fail again in its task, by concealing God as judge, and speaking of him only as physician.

By saying that he is unable to bear his punishment, Cain confesses his weakness, and lays it bare before God. No more arrogance! Humility comes to Cain's aid, dictating a truth to him. Cain is passion personified as his name states; when passion describes itself as weak, it is because it is humble. Humility is now able to become established in Cain's heart; it will hold him back from anger.

But the same phrase of Cain's is much richer in the Hebrew than our translation can say. Cain indeed speaks here of his punishment being too heavy to bear, but, in light of the multiple meanings of Hebrew words, he is also saying something else. Cain says:—

My guilt is too heavy to bear

The Hebrew word *awon* signifies "punishment," "fault," "sin," and "guilt." Cain says here that he has no strength to bear the weight of his guilt. This is a beaten down man who presents himself to God, crushed by the death of his brother, by the murder of the innocent. The anger has left Cain. It was with him to bring about the murder of Abel, and that was easy. Now it has left him alone to bear his fault, and it is too heavy.

My fault is too heavy to be borne

This is another valid translation.

Cain confesses his fault, the immensity of it. By confessing it to God, he sets himself on the road of repentance, just as the prodigal son sets out on the road of return, to present himself before his father. The most beautiful result possible would be forgiveness, forgiveness which God alone can give.

Certainly, Cain takes the road of repentance, but he knows very well that for him this road is a dead end, because forgiveness is impossible.

In effect, Cain is saying to God:—

My fault is too great to be forgiven

The Hebrew verb *nâsâ'*, which is translated here as "support" or "bear," also means "forgive," above all when dealing with a fault and when God is the verb's subject, this God who "forgives faults" (Exod 34:7).

Cain presents himself before the one who alone can forgive, but to tell him that "*my fault is too great to be forgiven,*" which is to say, "you can't forgive a failing as monstrous as mine." He had done worse than the prodigal son, and he too could say with good reason, "*I am not worthy to be called your son.*"

Indeed, the road of repentance may be open and Cain is on it, but he knows very well that there is no question of any hope of pardon. He is unworthy of it, unworthy even to hope for forgiveness.

Nevertheless, Cain is opening his heart to God. Even though despairing, he turns towards God; it is to him that he speaks and to him that he prays.

Cain has found the way of prayer: "Lord, I do not even ask pardon; my fault is too great. I simply open my heart to you for you to measure how great the fault is. I am not worthy to be called your son. I don't even know if I should speak to you as a judge or as a physician. I am unworthy of anything except the curse you have pronounced on me, and I don't have the strength to bear it . . ."

Then, before he departs to roam the earth, Cain adds to his prayer these words: "*Behold, you are chasing me today from this land; I will be hidden far from your face, I will be a wanderer and a vagrant on the earth, and whoever finds me will kill me.*"

Whoever finds me will kill me

This is the final word of Cain's first and last prayer; *"they will kill me!"*
And God listens . . .
He listens very closely . . .

With extreme care . . .

With the care of a father.

God responds to this prayer; he responds and steps in at once as judge, as physician, as a true spiritual father—quite simply, as God.

The Eternal placed a sign on Cain

"The Eternal said to him: Should anyone kill Cain, Cain will be avenged seven times over. And the Eternal placed a sign on Cain so that whoever encountered him would not kill him."
God's intervention is that of a judge who softens the penalty with a sign of protection. He decrees something akin to parliamentary immunity; no one is to kill Cain; the sign he wears is God's protection for him, the God who gives him life.

By this action God openly reveals the kind of judge he is, the kind of justice he applies. God's justice is to lift the weak; just as God raised Abel the weak by honoring his offering, he now raises Cain in his weakness by marking him with a protective sign. God's words and actions speak of his grace which saves Cain from death, of his love which brings life.

God's intervention is also that of a physician and initiates convalescence; he marks the convalescent with a sign so that others will make no attack on him in his weakness, on his life. From now on, Cain can live. You are weak, Cain, to be sure but the sign I place on you will be your strength; it will be my strength in you, for you.

The sign is one of alliance between God and Cain; an alliance in which God engages himself by a promise of protection, an eternal alliance. Healing is part of this agreement, a covenant of love in which God is so humble as to choose as his witness a pardoned murderer, a weak man, of whom he alone is the strength.

The spiritual father can recommit his son to the pathway of life with a sign of protection on him and a word of life in his heart. Cain has opened his heart and God has placed there a word of life.

Cain departs

"Cain went out from the presence of the Eternal and lived in the land of Nod, to the east of Eden." When we open our hearts to God it is not sin which comes in but the Holy Spirit, who makes his dwelling place there and deposits his gifts as his healing remedies: love, joy, peace, patience, kindness, goodness, faithfulness, gentleness, self-control . . .

Cain has his heart full of all this. He can wander the earth on the road to healing; his heart has become a temple, the temple of the Holy Spirit.

Eden is on the horizon.

Cain now lives by the grace and love of the Father.

— CHAPTER 3 —

The Fathers' Medicine

IT IS NOT POSSIBLE to review here all the biblical texts in which God appears in the role of physician, whether in the Old Testament or the New; neither is there space to examine the remarkable kinship there is between the comportment of Jesus towards the sick and that of God with Cain, though it is the same compassion, the same assurance, the same desire for full, radiant spiritual life.

Again, it is not possible to review each spiritual malady with a view to discerning its symptoms and to understanding its treatment, to follow the stages by which each one develops. I have neither the time nor the competence for this; my preference is to take a step back and take a more global view of the edifice the Fathers slowly constructed over the centuries, starting with the biblical data, and providing an overview of the range of spiritual maladies. This should help you to better understand this or that page of a Father you might read in which there is an issue of God as physician, or a person with a spiritual sickness.

The eight principal passions

The Fathers took time to go over all the spiritual maladies, to examine and analyze them, as much because of their being incident to themselves and their associates as for the sake of those who came to consult them. They spent time in prayer and meditation, the better to understand the maladies in the light of the Scriptures. They thus discovered links between the maladies, links similar to those of parentage; this enabled them to construct a sort of family tree, and so go back to the root maladies, those which originate the others and which, at the same time, are more pervasive and therefore more important too.

The Fathers concluded in distinguishing eight principal maladies, eight maladies so widespread and, in each case, virtually chronic that they found it correct to label them "passions," given that a passion is a malady that lies at the door of one's heart, so to speak, permanently. According to the Fathers, it is not that one is perpetually sick but that one is perpetually menaced by the maladies and above all by the eight principal ones.

If a person is not continually sick, this is a particular grace of baptism.[1] Baptism, in fact, accords a person a state of perfect well-being. The baptized person is no longer sick in the way they might have been before their baptism; they are nevertheless always subject to the maladies that may previously have assailed them; they will always be predisposed that way. In baptism, God heals us, without, nonetheless, having caused the disappearance of the maladies from the face of the earth. We might say today, that God heals us, without however causing the disappearance of microbes. We are healed, but the microbes continue their existence and our organism is always exposed and vulnerable to them.

Baptized persons therefore need to be extremely vigilant to avoid any relapse; they must not do anything foolish. For the Fathers there are three forms of indiscretion in the spiritual life: negligence, ignorance of God, and the forgetting of spiritual realities. A person who keeps their guard up and fights against these is a true "watchman." They have the passions subdued, with God's help.

---

1. It might be well to think here of baptism "into Christ." (Trans.)

Spiritual Maladies

We come now to the eight principal passions, which I will enumerate in a particular order; greed, lust, avarice, melancholy[2], laziness[3] (which is to say, a lack of taste for the spiritual life; we referred to it as depression at one point in the story of Cain; it was known to the Latins as sloth[4]), anger, vainglory, and pride.

In the West these eight passions have been reduced to seven following the assimilation of vainglory and pride into one malady. Further to this, these passions have been called the "seven deadly sins," a very juridical way of speaking of them. Where the Eastern church put the accent on the "medical" aspect by speaking of "passions," the Western placed its accent on the legal aspect with its reference to "sins"; this completely alters our position with regard to God, as we have said. "Sin" or "passion"; we see how the simple choice of words to speak of the same realities has important consequences.

The order in which I have just enumerated the passions is not the order in which we might "catch" the maladies, but it is the order in which we might discover them in ourselves. The first, greed, is the easiest to spot, and the last, pride, the most hidden (and dissembled). The first two give themselves away the most readily since they affect the whole body (greed and lust), where the others are more buried, more interiorized. We are not dealing with a classification that orders them in terms of their seriousness because each of them exists more or less in all of us.

You may have noted that selfishness[5] is not mentioned among the eight principal passions. This is because the Fathers didn't really consider it to be one; selfishness is seen rather as a sort of background color that is common to all of them; each malady has its imprint of self-centeredness.

---

2. In French, tristesse, which is sadness or dejection. (Trans.)

3. "Acedie"; this would be the Greek term; the author makes a distinction between the Greek and Latin Fathers; despondency. (Trans.)

4. "Sloth" being the traditional English translation. (Trans.)

5. Egoism, self-centeredness. (Trans.)

The three most important passions

Among the eight passions, the Fathers noted again links of parentage, which led them to regard three of them as giving birth to the others. These three are greed, avarice, and vainglory.

These three "parents" have in common their effect on our faculty of love. Our ability to love is sick when it is not directed towards God or our neighbor; this is the case whether we turn towards pleasure (this is greed), towards money (avarice), or towards glory and praise (vainglory). If these three passions are maladies of the love faculty, this says that each of their daughters will also, more or less, affect our ability to love. Each malady, in its various degrees, is, at its source, a disease of our love, which shows why it is so important it be tended, given that the whole of the Christian life is totally rooted in love.

When the Fathers speak of the love of pleasure, of money, or of glory as the three major maladies, it is not suggested that pleasure, money, or glory are bad in themselves; certainly not! Pleasure is good, as are money and glory; all of this is good; what is noxious is not the things as such but our exaggerated attachments to them. From the moment I am more attached to pleasure than I am to God or my neighbor, I am sick. From the moment I am more attached to money than I am to God or to my neighbor, I am sick, and the same with vainglory. In short, from the moment some attachment means more than our love for God or our neighbor it has become excessive. Thus, the malady is really nothing more than an excess; the malady lies in its excessiveness. Pleasure, money, and glory are wonderful gifts that God gives us for our good, and which we must learn to receive with thanksgiving and use appropriately. I trust this removes any misunderstanding about the teachings of the Fathers.

God created humanity as a being of desire; pleasure is found in whatever satisfies a desire. The number one desire is desire for God; as the psalmist says: "*My soul thirsts for you, my flesh longs after you*" (Ps 63:1). "My soul," "my flesh": the whole being of a person reaches out in total desire, a desire that God fulfills incomparably. The person who fully desires God will find what real pleasure is in God; they will also discover true desire for others, true pleasure with others, and every desire and pleasure that has God as its source. However, every pleasure sought outside desire for God is cut off from its source and quickly overreaches itself; this is when it becomes bad, noxious, and makes the person sick.

Money is also a gift from God, a blessing, but the danger is to love the gift of God more than God himself, the gift more than the giver. From the moment we prefer the gift to the giver, we are sick.

Glory or praise is also a benefit received from God. When he tells us that we are his children, a son or a daughter, we are receiving the glory of being honored by him as he fills us with his love and grace. But anyone who accords greater importance to some other glory than this is a person who is sick.

Generally speaking, we need to learn, with God's help, to let go of any excessive attachment, learn to receive from God all his gifts, knowing that they are destined to be returned to him as offerings or to be shared with our brothers and sisters. If our attachment to God does not outweigh every other attachment, then we are particularly vulnerable to the seduction of the beast that lies in wait at the door of our heart.

Christ, the vanquisher of the passions

The Fathers noted that the three principal passions are exactly the same as those that Jesus overcame in the wilderness during the temptation. Even Jesus has therefore been exposed like us to the seductiveness of the passions, though he kept himself from them. Jesus was exposed to greed when it was suggested he turn the stones into bread (Luke 4:3–4); to avarice, when the tempter proposed the kingdoms of the world as goods to be possessed (Luke 4:5–8); and to vainglory when it was suggested he throw himself down from the temple pinnacle, thereby bringing him glory in the eyes of the crowd (Luke 4:9–12). Jesus, however, was able to reject each suggestion, each seduction, thanks to his perfect attachment to God; he mastered the beast, and so kept himself from any malady. By overcoming the three principal passions, Jesus also vanquished each passion that derives from them. He alone is the true overcomer, the one in perfect health, and in our baptism we become beneficiaries of his triumphs. Each of our victories over the passions is none other than a participation in the victory of Christ who fights besides us, with us, in us, by his Spirit. This is what it means to be a beneficiary of Christ's victories, and without him we are already, subtly, sick with pride. In Christ, with him in us, we can have good spiritual health.

The most important of all

As they examined the three major passions, the Fathers concluded, in the light of the Bible, that avarice is the most important of the three. They reached this conclusion on the basis of the verse of Paul's that says *"The root of all evils[6] is the love of money"* (1 Tim 6:10). This verse helps us understand this saying of Jesus: *"No one can serve two masters; either he will hate one and love the other or else be attached to this and despise that. You cannot serve God and Mammon* [which is to say, money]" (Matt 6:24). In speaking like this, Jesus presents us with the primordial choice; to prefer God over Mammon is to resist all the maladies.

Complicity among the passions

The classification of passions drawn from the teaching of the Fathers requires some comment to avoid confusion.

---

6. "All evils" or "all kinds of evil," according to the Greek. (Trans.)

To speak of the passions having a parentage is a picture and rather approximate. Such parentage is not of a type to have a family tree, as if each malady had only one father and mother. The parentage the Fathers speak of is different; it's a kinship by which each passion could engender any other, making it impossible to draw up some one family tree. The better to understand this, we can leave that picture and turn to what Jesus said in a parable. *"When the unclean spirit is gone out of a man, it wanders through the desert regions seeking rest, but is unable to find it. Then it says to itself, I will return to my house which I have left; when it arrives it finds the place unoccupied, swept and put in order. Then it goes and takes with it seven other spirits worse than itself; they enter in and settle down. Thus the last state of the man is worse than the first"* (Matt 12:43–45).

This parable speaks of a total of eight unclean spirits (which is to say eight demons), which correspond to the eight passions. The parable doesn't name the eight spirits, but for the Fathers they are the eight principal passions. Jesus doesn't say which the first demon is which then brings in the others; the Fathers conclude from this that each demon acts the same way; each draws the others in behind it, which is why Jesus didn't name the first. This is a very just description. With Cain, the first demon was anger, and it was able to introduce the others. For each person, the first demon might be a different passion. Each one has sufficient authority with the others to introduce them. It is this authority relationship which causes the Fathers to speak in terms of parentage.

We need to understand this issue of parentage since it is an ever-present with the Fathers. They say further, to put the story of Cain alongside the Gospel parable, that each passion to which we open the door can bring the seven other principal passions right in behind it, and with them every other malady!

A person in good health is one in whom no malady is to be found, which is to say that his house is not occupied by any demon. The parable puts us on guard; a house which is "unoccupied, swept and in order" is the door which is open to all the demons! What could this mean except that the house must be occupied—but by whom if the demons are not to establish themselves? It must be occupied by God. A heart in which God dwells, this is good spiritual health.

We will pause now over this notion of good spiritual health.

Good spiritual health

God created humanity in good health. He made it good, which is to say inclined to love God, and, since genuine love flourishes in freedom, inclined to love him freely.

In creating humanity good, God created it *"in his image and likeness"* as Genesis specifies (1:26). To be in the image of God is to be a healthy person; but then we need to be precise about what this image of God means.

The particularity of God is that God both is and is becoming; God is a being who is eternally becoming, as the book of Revelation so wonderfully tells us: *"He is, he was and he is to come"* (Rev 1:4). These three phrases translate in themselves the proper name of God, that is, the name that reveals the mystery of his being. The proper Hebrew name of God, the well known "tetragram" (YHWH), which is never spoken but always replaced by the word "Lord," this name is beyond translation; nevertheless, the author of the Revelation, with the genius of inspiration, does render it with the words "he is, he was, he is to come." By indicating the substance of God's proper name, this phrase speaks of the profound being of God in all God's mystery. God "is," but not only now, in the present, but from all time ("he was"); God is becoming too, as is specified by "he is to come." "He is to come"; this is the becoming of God.

To just say that God "is" is not enough. This is said by Greek philosophy, but it is not biblical. God is, yes, but more precisely, God is a being who is becoming, both unchanging ("he is") and changing ("he is to come"). God "is" eternally, and never ceases to become.

The proper name of God, the Hebrew tetragram, is a form of the verb "to be" but such as to be incomplete; this shows perfectly that God is a being who is becoming.

Humanity in the image of God

If this is how God is, there could be no statue of him since a statue is something fixed, unmoving; it is not something that is becoming. A statue would be a caricature of God. By contrast, while God has no statue, he does have an unfixed image, one in movement, an image which is and becomes. This is humanity, made in the image of God.

Created good, humanity has well-being, but the intrinsic quality of this good health is to be in the image of God, which is to say, it is and it becomes; it is both given and is becoming, unceasingly already given by God, and unceasingly receiving from him. Good health, well-being, is a state but also a never completed process, always becoming; it is not a definitive acquisition, but one which becomes; we are created well and we never cease to become well. In short, good health is truly both "already" and "not yet." All this shows that our well-being is ceaselessly exposed to and menaced by sickness. It must continually be guarded.

The Fathers,to simplify, express all this in the following way: humanity is "*in the image and likeness*" of God; the image is the "already" of the well person; the likeness is the "not yet."

We need to keep hold of this; the well person is both already and not yet, in a process which cannot be pinned down; fixing it would transform the image into a statue; perhaps we should think in terms of paralysis!

Christ the image of God

We should also say, with regard to the image of God, that there does exist a model, a reference point, in the person of Jesus Christ. Christ is the image without equal, as stated by Paul to the Colossians (1:15) and to the Corinthians (2 Cor 4:4). He is the image *par excellence*, having resisted the seduction of the beast at the door as no one has ever resisted; in this regard we are all sick and he alone is well, though we realize, as Paul again tells us, that we are predestined to be conformed to the image of Christ (Rom 8:29).

As such, Christ being the image without equal, and we on the road to being like him, our attention turns to him to better understand in what exactly the image of God consists and what it is to be whole.

The expression "the image of God" is not one we find in Jesus' mouth to describe either us or him. On the other hand, he does say the following of himself, which conveys the same idea: "*He who has seen me has seen the Father*" (John 14:9). This, I believe, is a way of saying that Jesus is the image of the Father. Anyone who sees the image of God sees God.

After saying this, Jesus adds a phrase which specifies what it means to "be in the image": "*I am in the Father and the Father is in me*" (John 14:10).

I have found no truer definition of the image of God than this, but it is not an image which can be depicted; it is something so internal, being in God with God in us. We are dealing here with something doubly interior; deeply within people and deeply within God.

The image of God is described here as an interdependent relationship, and this is where our well-being is to be found; to be in God and God in us. Well-being, described like this, is a way of being, a way of becoming, a way of living which is inseparable from God; which is to say inseparably tied to God, inseparable from the Father, from the Son, and from the Holy Spirit.

SPIRITUAL MALADIES

The serpent's ruse

Sickness is an attack on this relation of interdependence; it is to not be in God, and God not to be in us; it is everything that warps, compromises, weakens, and perturbs this relationship. That's what sin is. Sin worms its seductive way in to break the unbreakable bond.

The serpent's whole ploy consisted in separating the inseparable with his subtle game. He put to one side "in God" to replace it with "like God." He is very careful not to say to humanity that they are in God, but suggests that they be like God. "*On the day in which you eat the fruit, your eyes will be opened and you will be like gods*" (Gen 3:5).[7] In this way the serpent's comments establish a distance between God and humanity.

To be "*like God*" is to be alongside God, at a distance from God, a distance sufficient to enable a comparison which will very quickly become a competition, a rivalry . . . Where there is any distance from God, there is sickness.

Man, filled with new dreams by the serpent, has preferred to be "like God" rather than "in God," and thus it has always been; humanity always at a distance from God, always sick.

Jesus repositions us with a perspective of well-being by proposing we be in God and he in us, of abiding in God, just as the Son is in the Father and the Father in the Son.

Well-being consists in love

To be in God and God in us; this is a way of defining a relationship of love, a most profound love, a true love, a love without confusion or separation, a love of communion, not one of fusion.[8]

---

7. Translations hesitate between "gods" and "God"; the French here is "gods." (Trans.)

8. Which would imply loss of identity. (Trans.)

To be in God and God in us; well-being consists in this profound relationship of love with God. This reinforces what the Fathers have said about spiritual maladies, that they are all, finally, sicknesses of our ability to love.

From the moment I become aware that God is not in me and that I am not in God, I discover that I am sick. Since this has to do with the very core of my life, with my love for God and for others, I discover my extreme need to keep careful watch over myself, the extreme need of coming before Christ to say to him, "Lord, heal me."

Robust spiritual health: our whole life depends on it, our love for God and for others, our witness, our obligations . . . everything! But is this something we are aware of? To say today that greed is a serious spiritual malady causes smiles . . . and yet it is just as serious as the anger in the story of Cain; just as serious as the other passions which eat away at our love, the heart of our lives.

In need of care

How can we see clearly when it comes to our duties if we are the blind leading the blind—when vainglory indeed makes us blind, as indeed does melancholy?

How can we hear the word of God if we are deaf—when anger stops up our ears?

What of our witness if we are sad, when the New Testament says we should always be joyful (1 Thess 5:16)?

How much damage have we done with a pretended love for our neighbor, when it is really a love vitiated by lust?

Why do we not join the crowd that presses around Christ to receive his healing?

I sometimes hear the answer given to these questions that it is not so serious, that there are no penalties attached. God is not going to punish us for our sadness! Punishment, sanctions; this is the typically

Western way of responding, intoning about the juridical, when what is in question is our well-being.

Again, I sometimes hear it said that we can count on God's grace to pardon. Here again, refuge is sought in terms of the tribunal when the real issue is a visit to the hospital. What good is there in endless forgiveness of a thief for his thefts; shouldn't we one day focus on his kleptomania in order to heal him of it?

To care about one's well-being is to care about the quality of one's love; it is to care about the gift of God. To offer love out of a sound heart, this is what it means to love God and one's neighbor.

Though we may not care very much about this, nonbelievers are very attentive. They are very often repulsed or scandalized by our diseased love; and they do not let us off lightly if our life is sickening with its infections.

We wind up becoming habituated to our maladies in the same way we become habituated to a corn on the foot which we have neglected; however, our spiritual maladies are altogether more serious! Who will say that anger is not serious after reading the story of Cain?

Lord Jesus, have pity on me and heal me! Come and make your dwelling place in me that I may dwell in you. Come and dwell in us that we may dwell in you. May our state of well-being finally be such as to fulfill your own prayer; that, as you ask of the Father, we may be in you as you are in him, and he in you, that the world may believe that the Father has sent you (John 17:21).

Some remarks on diagnosis

While there are only eight principal passions, there are a host of others which follow in behind them; these are more or less serious, but there are a large number of them all the same, hundreds according to the lists drawn up by the Fathers. This is a substantial matter, and the question that arises is for us to know, when we are sick, by which malady we are affected. We need a diagnosis, which is to say, in more spiritual terms, discernment.

Discernment is indispensable if we are to establish a diagnosis. This discernment comes from God, a gift of the Holy Spirit. We will never be able to discern matters alone, by ourselves; we necessarily require the help of God, of his Holy Spirit. No gift becomes a permanent possession; it always stands in need of being renewed, of being received afresh, always changing; so, if we are to discern, we must continually abide in God.

God certainly knows our condition exactly, good physician that he is; he is the one who "tries the reins and the heart,"[9] the one who knit us together in our mother's womb, so there is no need to insist on this point.

God does at times cure us of some maladies without telling us, but it is better if we ourselves are aware of them, the better to participate in the necessary treatment, and also the better to appreciate the well-being God brings. We are constantly called to witness to the work of God within us; if we are to participate in this work as witnesses to it, this too is a matter for discernment.

When God draws our attention to one of the maladies, he does so with wonderful tact, as we saw in the case of Cain. God is a physician who overflows with love, a remarkable teacher.

God also has the knack of showing us our maladies little by little, one at a time, not all at once, so that we are not tempted to despair; just enough to mobilize us and excite our collaboration. When we emerge from one concern, he draws our attention to another malady we had not yet noted, buried as it had been; the physician's work proceeds, always deeper. God arranges things so as always to be showing us something a little beyond our ability so that we don't pass him over and fall into that most tenacious of our faults, pride. What a wonderful physician! He understands the rhythm of our walk towards healing, the intensity of light we are able to bear. This is how he leads us, keeping us both from

---

9. Psalm 26:2. (Trans.)

pride and from discouragement, all the while encouraging our love and humility; we could find no better physician than him.

God helps us discern our own maladies rather than those of our neighbor, even if they are undergoing a violent crisis of some sort—though this is altogether another topic, and one we will not go into. Our starting place, with God's help, is to consider the beam in our own eye before we try removing the specks from the eyes of our neighbors! I say this to restrain the zeal of those who are discovering a vocation as healers; we may feel ready to heal the ills of humanity, but we need first to give ourselves over to the care and cure that God will administer.

What are the signs God gives to help us in our discernment? I will indicate a few of those the Fathers received from God and have handed on.

Perhaps you become distracted when you pray, and no doubt these distractions are humiliating. I can readily understand because I experience the same thing. Well, such distractions are precisely a place from which we can draw great profit—not that we should entertain the distractions, but rather examine them in a new light.

When you feel this way, analyze a little the sort of thoughts that arise and you will quickly discover that they are always somewhat similar. Your thoughts might stray mostly in the direction of food, or of money, or of the other sex . . . which is to say that these distractions will show which malady is most active within you, greed, avarice, lust . . . in line with the thoughts we have just listed. This is a most precious aid to discernment; distractions are doubly precious, enabling us to discern our trouble and keeping us humble.

Alongside distractions like this, we find dreams; sexual fantasies inhabit the dreams of someone suffering from lust; a proud person will often dream of himself with wings on his back or seated on a throne. But I won't insist on this since it is all well known, much better known than the matter of distractions during prayer.

Diagnosis may also be facilitated by day-to-day events; not by the events themselves, but by the way we react to them. We can give an example from which we can draw our own conclusions. If the woman who lives in the house across the road sits in her window somewhat scantily clad, how do you react? Do you close your window? Do you go out onto the balcony? Or perhaps you fetch your binoculars?

Bible reading is certainly a wonderful help along our way to discernment, both because it holds up before us a picture of wholeness, and because it depicts the maladies. In both cases there is great profit. Everything we see in Christ helps us measure our own failings; maladies like that of Cain also illuminate our condition. Often just one word of Christ's is enough for us to understand the gravity of something we had considered anodyne. In the Sermon on the Mount, for example, Jesus helps us see clearly within ourselves when it comes to the question of lust: "*Whoever looks on a woman with desire has already, in his heart, committed adultery with her*" (Matt 5:28). It is up to us to profit diagnostically from this verse.

Alongside the Bible, other spiritual writings are available to bring insight. *The Ladder of Divine Ascent* by John Climacus is very fine on this subject except that it might cause hypochondriacs to lose sleep! Even here, with reading like this, we must ask the help of the Holy Spirit in discerning the real state of our heart; for this, the company of a brother or sister can be a real gift from God, and it is on this last point that we will close our discussion of diagnosis.

It is difficult to see clearly on our own. God will help us with this, and his help might well take the form in a most profitable way of a brother or sister; when there are two the way becomes much easier. Not only can a brother or sister help by their contributions but can also help keep us from the pride of supposing that we can manage without others . . .

These are just a few remarks that I can pass on from the Fathers' teaching.

When Jesus found himself with a sick person who was seeking his help, his way was to ask, "*What do you wish me to do for you?*" (Luke 18:41). Happy are they who can say precisely what their difficulty is.

About remedies

The remedies are very various, firstly because the maladies are so numerous, but also because, for the same malady, the remedies vary as a function of how advanced it is; and again, because each malady is linked to the others in multiple combinations. The anger of a greedy person is not the anger of the avaricious or proud person . . . Each sort of anger has its own remedy, so again there is the question of discernment.

That said, there are some remedies that it is good to know as being of value for a great number of maladies. For example, all the maladies that affect the desire have temperance as a remedy; all those affecting the passion[10] will be remediated by courage; and those which affect the reason are treated with prudence.

Among the remedies that treat a range of maladies, there are two which are valuable in all cases, and we have already mentioned these; they are love and humility. With these two remedies everything can be healed, though we must not forget that love itself can be diseased should we at any time propose to do without God. When it comes to humility, it has the peculiarity of needing an infinity of time and care if we are to know how, not to acquire, but to welcome it, since it is a gift. Humility is a little like a transplant, and not any transplant—it is a new heart! For this remedy, there is nothing you can do of yourself except put yourself entirely in the hands of him who says he is lowly of heart and who calls out to us, "*Come to me, all you who are weary . . . because I am meek and lowly of heart*"(Matt 11:28–29).

All the remedies are given by God, who gives to those who ask, and at times even to those who don't, great as his love is. Ask all the same, Jesus counsels, but ask simply, without repetition, "*because your Father knows what you need before ever you ask*" (Matt 6:8).

God gives and also personally regulates the dosage according to each one's needs. To take a remedy in excess is also a malady! "*Your

---

10. As above, *ardeur*, the inner fire, the motivational force. (Trans.)

Father knows what you have need of also means that he knows the correct dose.

The whole of the Torah is a veritable pharmacy where an impressive array of remedies is to be found. Each article of the Law can perform the office of a cure. We said a little about that in the first chapter so we won't go back there; instead I would like to point out the way this is present in the Sermon on the Mount. The sermon is often received as though it were a new legal code, thereby forgetting its therapeutic dimension. A few remarks on this subject . . .

The Sermon on the Mount is found in Matthew's Gospel at an extremely significant point, right at the outset of Jesus' ministry; exactly in fact at the moment when he is about to acquire extraordinary fame as a healer. The end of chapter 4 of Matthew insists on this point (4:23–25); next, immediately after the sermon, chapter 8 describes in detail an imposing sequence of healings: that of a leper (8:1–4), the centurion's servant (8:5–13), Peter's mother-in-law, and then, so as not to tire the reader, Matthew gives us a sort of et cetera, saying that "*he healed all the sick.*" Have you ever seen a doctor who "healed all the sick"?

This is the context in which we find the Sermon on the Mount and so we are invited to understand it as issuing from the mouth of a healer. It was a physician the crowds followed up to the mountain; it is to him they entrusted their sick, and to him that they listened.

I will leave you to read over the sermon yourself; you will see that it contains a wealth of advice of a healing nature which will help both in diagnosis and as a prescription with its expert recommendations. To what is your brother's sin compared? To a speck of dust in the eye. This is the language of the hospital not the tribunal. As for the beam, this is hyperbole to say that emergency services and intensive care are required! There is one remedy, both curative and preventative: "*Don't judge!*" (Matt 7:1)

As a good healer, Jesus knows exactly what remedy suits each case. We might note the account of the rich young man. He is sick, a troubled person who knows himself to be sick, but doesn't know what his trouble is. He had tried all the remedies of the Torah but without success, which is why he says to Jesus, *"What must I do to have real life?"* In reply, Jesus first of all checks that the man has been following the prescriptions of the Law, then he gives the only medication suitable for the problem he discerns. The man's sickness is avarice; the medication is a sort of emetic; *"Go, sell all that you have, give it to the poor, and then come and follow me"* (Matt 19:21). If these words of Jesus were somehow a law, they would apply to everyone, but Jesus did not say this to all his disciples, only to those in whom he discerned avarice. This is a medication given with love, as Mark notes (*"looking on him, he loved him"* 10:21); and a medication which works with the violence of love. However, the young man was unable to discern the love; all he saw was the violence of the purgative. He went away *"very sad,"* Matthew concludes (19:22). Avarice went to seek its neighbor, sadness, to take up residence in the man's home.

God also provides us with medicine through the events of life. We spoke above of the things that can help us discern, but we must realize too, that events can also at times work as remedies. It's precious to remember this when it comes to events that are painful and full of sorrow for us. They sting like alcohol on a wound; they are painful, but after a while, short or long, we can see the way events produced a healing effect. For the avaricious person, every loss of money is experienced as a catastrophe, when really there is matter in it to bring healing.

The synergy of healing

It is not a possible for a person to treat himself alone, either in terms of diagnosis or in establishing some healing regimen. It is God alone who treats and heals. Anyone who wishes to treat himself alone is sick with pride. But, you might say, you can take an aspirin without consulting a doctor! Well, yes, but this is not a spiritual medicine. Plainly a gourmand knows that he or she needs to guard against undisciplined eating, just as the angry person has to guard against snapping back in response to the slightest denigratory word; but even here, each of these simple remedies must be put into action with God's help. If you are angry and someone says something disobliging, invoke God's help to hold you back; without this, if you think to escape alone from the talons of anger, you will fall into the clutches of pride!

A remedy has its effect if the sick person believes in it, as we well know. If a patient is completely clammed shut internally against the remedy they are taking, it won't have the effect expected by the doctor. The same applies to the spiritual life; for healing, the sick person's faith is of great importance. This is why Jesus continually said to those he healed, "*Your faith has made you whole*" (Luke 8:48, 17:19, 18:42, as well as 7:50).

Jesus didn't say this to those who had healed themselves, but to those he had healed. Nevertheless, he said, "Your faith has healed you," never, "I have healed you."

This way of speaking of Jesus' evidences his perfect humility, but it also demonstrates what we might call the synergy of healing. The healing is the work of Christ, God's work, but it calls for and involves faith as the human participation in the work. Yes, a participation that is very minor since our faith is itself a gift of God, but a human participation all the same since, in the faith, there is a human element: our assenting, our acquiescence, our "yes" to the faith received, the "yes" to healing, the "yes" to the prescription, the "yes" to the opening of the heart to God's intervention. It is a "yes" despoiled of all pride, a "yes" in the image of the one who humbly tells us, "*your faith has made you whole*"; a "yes" that replies to him, "Lord, you know, it is you and you alone who have saved me," and will say to itself, "*Bless the Lord, O my soul, who heals your every disease*" (Ps 103:3).

The workings of sin

Sin, as an evil action, concerns the judge; but we know that sin is also tied to the underlying malady which needs to be treated.

Sin can be an occasional, chance, passing act . . . In this case the Fathers are generally very indulgent, inclined to simply forgive. They don't pay much attention to the occasional sin. In contrast, they are very attentive to a sin which is repeated and becomes habitual since this is the sign of a passion, the more difficult to heal as it is more engrained. In order to help heal the passions, the Fathers made efforts to explore the mechanism of sin from its origin in the passion to the point where it issues in the sinful action.

Before it is acted out, a passion has a pathway it follows at the level of the thoughts, in the heart. It is therefore important to intervene as early as possible in this process if it is to be checked.

An evil act stems from an evil thought, but not all thoughts are evil; happily there are good ones too. When the Fathers look at the thoughts, we mustn't be mistaken; they are talking only about the evil ones. It is these we will now discuss and these alone. Good thoughts are those we have as we abide in God.

What then of evil thoughts? The Fathers have distinguished different stages in the process of thought that they describe as follows: first, there is suggestion (this is where the beast which lies at the door of the heart begins; it starts with a suggestion), then comes the welcome (when the person listens to the suggestion which comes from the outside), then there is discussion (an internal dialogue with the thought received), then acquiescence (when I accept the seducer's thought as my own), before finally passing on to the act.

What shall we say about this? The longer I wait before reacting, the harder it becomes to resist; the thought is a like a leech that gains more and more strength the more attention I accord it. The Fathers have a very beautiful image to illustrate this growing difficulty in the fight against an evil thought. The Fathers in question, for the most part, were monks living in the desert in Egypt or elsewhere. A thought, they say, is like a snake which had entered their cell through a hole in the wall. If the snake is spotted as soon as its head alone is poking through hole it is easy to kill, if you react without delay. If you do delay, the struggle becomes difficult; the longer you delay, the harder it gets.

In the progress of a thought, we cannot speak of sin in the juridical sense until a particular moment, that of acquiescence. Until then, the suggestion, the reception, and the discussion are not sins that can be laid to our account; up to this point it is the fault solely of the beast. That is to say, the fact that a thought presents itself to us, without our acquiescence, is not something to be confessed as sin before the judge. On the contrary, this same thought, lacking our complicity, is to be brought into the open before the physician as the symptom of a malady. Indeed, a thought, in its stage of suggestion, enables the diagnosis of some malady that is attacking us.

All this is very important. It allows us to remove condemnation from someone who believes themselves guilty for an evil thought that tracks across their spirit; this is not a culpable act. We can hold a discussion in our heart with some evil thought and be guilty of nothing if the thought is rejected. Someone who commits adultery in his heart (Matt 5:28) is guilty because his lust has caused him to acquiesce in the thought and effectively commit adultery in his imagination. Someone, however, who thinks about adultery without lust, examines the possibility and rejects it, does not commit adultery in their heart. They are not to be condemned. On the contrary, they are to be praised for repelling the temptation.

When the Fathers speak of and examine in this way the process of thought and the moment when thought becomes sin, they do so after close observation of the behavior of the one who didn't sin, Christ. The clearest account on this issue is the temptation. In his discussion with the tempter, Jesus underwent part of the process. The suggestion lay in the words the tempter spoke to Jesus; the reception, in Jesus' listening to them; and the discussion follows in Jesus' replies. But Jesus went no further; the replies give no place to any agreement. Knowing that Jesus never sinned, we see clearly at what moment a thought becomes sin and how far it can go before that happens.

In her conversation with the serpent, Eve did not sin by entering a discussion, not by listening to the suggestion, but by making the serpent's proposition her own.

Sin does not come from ourselves since it is suggested to us by another; but it plainly pertains to us in the degree to which we fall in with its suggestions. Where there is a synergy of healing in the acquiescence of faith, there is also a synergy of sin in our agreement with the tempter.

The dynamics of healing

The process of sin is a dynamic one in so far as there are certain forces at play, as we have seen in the story of Cain. We now need to speak about healing, and we will see that it too is dynamic, involving different forces.

The Evangelist Luke is known to have been a doctor and he accordingly peppers his writings with little notes on healing which are very precious.

In Luke 6:19 we read: "*The crowds sought to touch Jesus because a power (dunamis) went out of him and healed them all.*" This verse is very clear; healing comes from a power that is in Christ. For this reason we can speak of healing as a dynamic process since it brings into play a force with which Jesus is invested.

When the woman with the hemorrhage touched Jesus' garment, she was healed "*that very moment,*" Luke tells us (8:44), also specifying that it was known to Jesus: "*I felt power,*" he said, "*go out of me*" (8:46).

We see then that the power of healing which is found in Jesus is effective by contact. The verb "touch" is common to 6:19 and 8:44–47. Whether Jesus speaks or not, contact with him is enough to heal (cf.

Matt 8:15, where Jesus heals Peter's mother-in-law by touch without speaking to her). That said, whether Jesus makes this kind of gesture or not, his word alone is also enough to heal; it too is dynamic, as one man confesses, saying to him, "*Speak the word only and my servant will be healed*" (Luke 7:7). Jesus speaks with power (*dunamis*) and the demons leave (Luke 4:36), which is healing.

In short, Jesus' power is in both actions and words, and it heals. His whole being is so invested with it that even his garments heal.

The power that operates in Jesus is not one of which he is the source and that he holds on to as his own. The power is tied to the Holy Spirit, and comes from God; as Luke says, "*God anointed Jesus of Nazareth with the Holy Spirit and power*" (Acts 10:38). In short, the power is given by the Father to the Son in the Holy Spirit; it is the power of the Trinity, the power of life, power that heals. Jesus never held on to this power as a personal belonging; it is in him because he is in the Father, and the Father is in him. It is power by participation for anyone who is also in God and has God in him: power for life, from which flow healing and well-being.

Here is Acts 10:38 again: "*God anointed with the Holy Spirit and power Jesus of Nazareth, who went about from place to place doing good and healing . . .*" Healing is justly set in relation with divine power, but the rest of the verse is also very interesting because of the expression Luke uses to designate infirmities. He says: "*Jesus healed all those who were under the power (dunamis) of the devil.*" Opposed to the power of the Son received from the Father in the Spirit is the power of Satan, which is the power that causes sickness, the "*power of death,*" says Hebrews 2:14.

These then are the real forces in play: sickness is a manifestation of a dynamic process whose power is the power of death that comes from the devil; healing is a manifestation of a dynamic process whose power is the power of life which comes from the trinitarian God. Whoever is in God is alive, animated by the dynamic process of healing and life.

This power of life is such that those who are in God are healed of their sicknesses by his grace, but more, they are the carriers of healing to others. This is what the evangelists tell us too. Jesus received from his Father the power that heals, but he doesn't leave it there—he gives the disciples the same power too: "*Jesus gave his disciples power to heal*" (Luke 9:1). No more than it is an appurtenance of Christ is this power something that belongs to the disciples (Acts 3:12). It is in the disciples, received by them, working through them to the degree that they are in God and God in them. It is a power working by participation, in a communion of love with God.

The disciples also have power over all the power of the enemy (Luke 10:19); they also heal the sick with a touch (Acts 3:7); but all the while they heal, they efface themselves before the truth and say "Jesus heals you" (Acts 9:34), because it is indeed Jesus who heals through the disciples.

Such is a true disciple, one who abides in Christ, and humbly effaces himself before him, saying, "*Jesus heals you; take up your bed and walk.*"

The Prayer of Bartimaeus

Seigneur Jésus; je te rends grâce.
Le jour pour moi ressemblait à la nuit;
J'avais la main tendue sur un bord de fossé
Et les gens par pitié me donnaient à manger.
Mais personne n'a su que j'avais soif d'amour
Et que mon cœur aveugle ne savait pas aimer.
Mon cœur aussi mendiait dans la nuit.

Seigneur Jésus, je te rends grâce.
Toi seul as su poser ton regard sur mon cœur;
Toi seul as découvert combien j'étais malade.
Alors j'ai pu te demander de me donner de voir
Pour quitter le fossé et marcher sur tes pas.

Seigneur Jésus, je te rends grâce.
En me donnant de voir, tu as touché mon cœur;
Tu l'as ouvert à une autre lumière;
C'est pourquoi maintenant je reste à tes côtés:
En toi rayonne la véritable lumière.

Seigneur Jésus, je te rends grâce.
Tu me fais découvrir un grand nombre d'aveugles;
Tu fais jaillir en moi une source d'amour.
Garde mon cœur ouvert aux mendiants de la route
Pour donner avec toi ce dont tu me combles.

Lord Jesus, I give you thanks.
The day to me resembled night,
As from the side of the road I stretched out
    my hand
And in pity people gave into my need.
But no one knew of my thirst for love,
That my blind heart's capacity for love was gone,
That my heart too was pleading in darkness.

Lord Jesus, I give you thanks.
You alone knew to look into my heart;
You alone could see my true sickness.
I asked you to give me my sight,
To leave the ditch and to follow you.

Lord Jesus, I give you thanks.
In giving me sight, you touched my heart;
You have opened me up to another light,
Which is why now I stay at your side:
For in you shines the light that is true.

Lord Jesus, I give you thanks.
You lead me to others who are equally blind;
You cause a fountain of love to open within me.
Keep my heart open to the needy I meet
To give them, with you, what fills me.

Spiritual Maladies

Seigneur Jésus,
La nuit et encore aux aguets;
Elle se tient couchée sur le pas de ma porte.
O toi, Jésus, lumière sans déclin,
Veille avec moi sur mon cœur
Ainsi que sur la source dont tu as le secret.

Seigneur Jésus, je te rends grâce.
Toi dont le seul désir est d'habiter en nous
Pour que nous demeurions en toi
Et dans le Père et dans l'Esprit,
Dans un bonheur sans fin,
Un amour sans limite.

Lord Jesus,
The night is still watching;
It stays crouched by my door.
O Jesus, light undeclining,
Watch with me over my heart,
The fountain of which you are the secret.

Lord Jesus, I give you thanks.
You, whose only desire is to live in us
So that we may dwell always in you,
In the Father, and Spirit,
In joy unending,
Love without limit.

www.ingramcontent.com/pod-product-compliance
Lightning Source LLC
Chambersburg PA
CBHW030050100426
42734CB00038B/999